The Meaning of Church Membership

By WAYNE C. CLARK

VALLEY FORGE

JUDSON PRESS

THE MEANING OF CHURCH MEMBERSHIP

Fifteenth Printing, 1971

International Standard Book No. 0-8170-0103-4

Contents

Foreword

SOME of you who pick up this book have recently made a momentous decision. You have decided that you will become a Christian. You feel that God has been inviting you to do this, and that now you are ready to accept his Son, Jesus Christ, as your Savior and Lord. You want to declare your lifelong allegiance to him, and you desire to become a member of the church which he established in the world. Your reading of these six chapters—they are neither long nor difficult—will help you understand more fully what it means to be a Christian and a church member.

Perhaps you have already declared your faith in Christ and your readiness to follow him; perhaps you have already been received into the membership of the church. Even so, you can find profit in this brief book, for it sets forth for your benefit both your privileges and your responsibilities as a church member. It will answer many of the questions which no doubt are in your mind.

It may be that some of you who read these pages became a Christian many years ago. You may have united with the church when you were quite young. With the passing of the years, you have gained added understanding of the Christian life. Church membership has become more meaningful to you. Yet you, too, will welcome the opportunity to think again of all that is involved in becoming a Christian and a church member. A review of these matters cannot fail to increase your devotion to Christ. It will put into your heart a song of gratitude for God's many blessings. It will give you courage for whatever the day may bring.

Although this book has been written with the practices of Baptist churches in mind, it is believed that much of the treatment is sufficiently general to be helpful to those looking forward to membership in churches of other denominations.

CHAPTER I

So You Want to Join the Church

Becoming a Christian

Becoming a Christian is not something one does as casually as one selects a new hat or frock. There must be on the person's part a deep and genuine desire to become a Christian. A person becomes a Christian because he feels his life would be very incomplete without Jesus Christ as his Master and Savior. He becomes a Christian because he has experienced a sense of sin and loss. He becomes a Christian because he wants to leave behind forever the things which would hinder him in realizing the fullness of life. He wants his sins forgiven and his future made secure. He wants a power dwelling within him that will enable him to live victoriously.

Having felt this deep and persistent need, he turns to Jesus Christ in an act of complete surrender. Becoming a Christian is, first of all, an act of surrender to Jesus Christ. Although this may seem an act of weakness, it is not; it is an act of strength. You must surrender your will, your mind, your soul, and your body to Jesus Christ. You must pray: "Lord Jesus, take all of me there is. Here is my will; make it thy will. Here is my mind; fill it with heavenly wisdom. Here is my soul; renew it and cleanse it with thy truth. Here are my abilities; use them in thy service. Have mercy upon me, O Lord, and save me."

Now, grasp this great, central truth: we are saved, not by our goodness, because it is faulty; not by rituals and ceremonies, because in themselves they accomplish nothing. We are saved simply and solely by our faith in the Lord Jesus Christ. "For by grace you have been saved through faith," Paul reminded the Ephesians; "and this is not your own doing, it is the gift of God—not because of works, lest any man should boast" (Eph. 2:8-9). Read this verse over and over, until you have it fixed forever in your mind. Salvation it not obtained through good deeds, but through faith. "He saved us,"

5

Paul affirmed, "not because of deeds done by us in righteousness, but in virtue of his own mercy, by the washing of regeneration and renewal in the Holy Spirit" (Titus 3:5). In other words, salvation is not secured by the washing of water in baptism, but only by that cleansing which comes to the soul when the Holy Spirit of God is admitted into the throne-room of one's heart.

Salvation is by faith alone, and faith is surrender. It is the movement of the whole being toward God through Jesus Christ. Faith is more than merely believing with the mind that God is, was, and always shall be; it is more than acknowledging that Jesus actually was a historical person. That is simple assent of the mind. The faith that saves and renews the inner being is the faith that opens the door of the heart where Jesus has been waiting and knocking, and which says, "Come into my heart, Lord Jesus." Faith is more than accepting with one's mental processes the fact that once upon a time Jesus lived on earth. It is the acceptance of him and of what he taught into the very core of one's being.

Now that we have made some progress in discussing the initial step in the Christian life, let us talk for awhile on the subject of conversion. Quite probably you think at once of Paul's experience on the Damascus road, where he saw a great light, was struck to the ground, and heard a voice from heaven. And you are thinking: "What a marvelous, inspiring experience he had! I wish I could have one just like it. Unless I have such an experience, how shall I know that I have been saved?" A lot of people think the same thing, for preachers sometimes make the mistake of referring only to that type of conversion experience. They are always telling about someone's sudden and dramatic religious experience, and that tends to discourage those who have not had, and cannot have, a similar experience.

The fact is that there are many different ways in which one may have a conversion experience. Paul's way is one. Many, like Paul, have been changed in a moment of time; but on the other hand, many people have been genuinely converted whose experience, while wonderful, was quiet and gradual. For example, note the way in which some of Jesus' first disciples responded to his call. "Follow me," he said, and they quietly left their nets and followed him (Matt. 4:18-22). "Zacchaeus," he announced, "I must stay at your house today." After spending a few hours talking in his own home with the Master, Zacchaeus—the grasping, selfish, little-souled business-man—declared: "Behold, Lord, the half of my goods I give to the poor; and if I have defrauded any one of anything, I restore it fourfold" (Luke 19:1-10). On the road to Gaza, Philip, the evangelist, saw an imposing retinue of travelers approaching. He perceived that the leader of the group was an Ethiopian, a man of authority, and that he was reading as he rode in his chariot. Philip felt led of God to hail the man and talk with him. He found that the man was reading the writings of the prophet Isaiah. In response to the man's inquiry, Philip explained that the prophet, in the passage which the man was reading, had reference to Jesus Christ. He then proceeded to tell the Ethiopian more about our Lord. In this incident there is no suggestion of anything at all sensa-tional, but we know that the traveler was converted, for when they came to water he exclaimed: "See, here is water! What is to prevent my being baptized?" Philip baptized him, and then they both went their separate ways (Acts 8:26-40). It is just as scriptural and just as effective to be converted quietly as it is to be converted spectacularly.

My own conversion was of this quiet nature. I was a lad of about twelve years. Meetings were being conducted in our town by a visiting evangelist. I had been reared in the church, and my parents were faithful in the performance of their reli-gious obligations; but at that time I felt an awakening of some-thing within me that I had not been aware of before. I felt I needed to accept Jesus Christ as my personal Savior. Though but a boy, I felt a weight upon my soul, but I was afraid to respond to the evangelist's call to accept Christ. I think if my mother or my father had suggested it, I would have responded, but they did not, and I was not sure that the invitation to accept Jesus was intended for children. Finally, an elderly lady whom I did not know, and have not known since, noticed me and asked if I would not like to give myself to Jesus. Of course I would, and in a few minutes I was on my knees, confessing my faith in Jesus. As a result of that surrender, which in my boyish way was absolutely sincere and complete, there came to my soul a sense of satisfaction and spiritual peace. My conversion was not of the dramatic type such as might halt a hardened sinner in his course, but it was genuine and full of meaning to me.

The late Dr. George W. Truett, for many years the honored president of the Baptist World Alliance, stated that he was quietly converted one day, when as a boy he said, "I surrender now to Jesus Christ." Most of the people who belong to the churches were converted when they were children just entering adolescence. At that time of life there is a turning to God which is as natural as the opening of fresh, budding flowers to the morning sun.

If a child has been reared rightly, he will want to give his life to Jesus and to join the church. Sometimes we hear it said that a child should wait until he is older before joining the church, that then he will understand better what he is doing. It has been my observation and experience that we understand some things better as children than as adults; as children we may feel our spiritual need and the reality of God more keenly than when we are adults.

Viewed from the human side, conversion means turning from sin to God. It means making an about-face. As suggested in the parable of the prodigal son (Luke 15), it means coming to oneself and turning toward the Heavenly Father. It means a change in the way one thinks. The original word for "repent"—the word which both John the Baptist and Jesus used—is *metanoeite;* which means, literally, "change your mind." Conversion is such a change. It is more than merely being sorry for one's sins; it is being sorry enough to turn away from them. Conversion produces an elevation in one's life. It means putting out of the life the things that should not be there; it means letting into the life the things that should be there. The change which then is wrought in the believer's life by the grace and power of God is so wonderful that it is described as a "new birth" or, as the words are sometimes translated, a "birth from above" (John 3:3-8). "If then you have been raised with Christ, seek the things that are above, where Christ is, seated at the right hand of God. Set your mind on things that are above, not on things that are on earth. For you have died, and your life is hid with Christ in God" (Col. 3:1-3).

Joining the Church

Now that we have discussed somewhat that which takes place within you in the conversion experience, let us think for awhile about what it is you are expected to do in becoming a member of a church.

You ought to declare your intentions openly. In many churches, an opportunity to do this is provided in what we term the "invitation." The pastor often says a few words of invitation at the conclusion of his message, and those present are given an opportunity to express their desire to become Christians and members of the church. You may indicate this by going forward and being received by the pastor. Perhaps the pastor already has discussed with you rather fully the significance and responsibilities of the Christian life. If he has not done so, he may invite you to join with other new converts in a class in which you will be given instruction concerning the Christian life and concerning the duties and privileges of church members. This class may meet for several sessions.

A conference with the deacons may follow. In this conference you may be asked to tell why you have accepted Christ and wish to unite with the church. If the deacons are assured of your understanding and sincerity, they will recommend to the church that it vote to accept you as a candidate for baptism and thereafter to welcome you as a church member. In some churches it may be that the invitation is not given in so public a way, and that some other method of receiving new members is followed. If such is the case, the pastor will explain it to you.

At any rate, you must not hesitate to make an open declaration of your faith in Jesus Christ and of your intention to live the Christian life. Such a public profession puts you on record before God, before others, and before your own conscience as sincerely desiring to be numbered with God's people. "For man believes with his heart and so is justified," stated Paul, "and he confesses with his lips and so is saved" (Rom. 10: 10). Every one who acknowledges me before men," said Jesus, "the Son of Man also will acknowledge before the angels of God; but he who denies me before men will be denied before the angels of God" (Luke 12:8-9).

Let us remember also that to be forgiven our sins we must confess them. "If we confess our sins," wrote John, "he is faithful and just, and will forgive our sins and cleanse us from all unrighteousness" (1 John 1:9). This does not mean the confession of our sins to a priest. The New Testament in no place counsels us to confess our sins to any earthly priest. The only way in which it suggests confession of sin to a mortal being is the way which James recommends: "Therefore confess your sins to one another, and pray for one another, that you may be healed" (James 5:16). This refers to the act of confessing our sins to the one or ones we have wronged and seeking their forgiveness. This kind of confession will ease our soul of a burden that can be removed in no other way. However, to obtain divine forgiveness we are to confess our sins to God, for in the last analysis sin is an act against God. David prayed:

> "Against thee, thee only, have I sinned,
> And done that which is evil in thy sight."
> —*Psalm 51:4*

Jesus is our great High Priest (Heb. 4:14-16) who sits at God's right hand interceding for us (Heb. 7:25).

Accepting a Christian Way of Life

We have thought about surrender, faith, and confession; let us now consider what an acceptance of the Christian way of life really means.

In joining the church, you are undertaking to follow a way of life that is distinctively Christian. This is fundamental. All the depths of the Christian life are not sounded in moral conduct, but the life you will be trying to live will not be Christian unless it recognizes Christian standards of moral conduct. The Christian faith is a religion of deeds, not of ideas merely.

Jesus Christ was primarily a man of action, and his emphasis was on action. "You will know them by their fruits," he declared. "Not every one who says to me, 'Lord, Lord,' shall enter the kingdom of heaven, but he who does the will of my Father, who is in heaven. . . . Every one then who hears these words of mine and does them will be like a wise man who built his house upon the rock; and the rain fell, and the floods came, and the winds blew and beat upon that house, but it did not fall, because it had been founded on the rock. And every one who hears these words of mine and does not do them will be like a foolish man who built his house upon the sand; and the rain fell, and the floods came, and the winds blew and beat against that house, and it fell; and great was the fall of it" (Matt. 7:20-27).

Jesus was no dreamy-eyed, philosophical visionary. He was an intensely practical man of action. "Why do you call me 'Lord, Lord,' and not do what I tell you?" he asked searchingly (Luke 6:46).

On another occasion, he declared: "My mother and my brothers are those who hear the word of God and do it" (Luke 8:21).

After the conference with the woman at the well in Samaria, he said to his disciples, "My food is to do the will of him who sent me, and to accomplish his work" (John 4:34).

To his disciples he said: "You are my friends if you do what I command you" (John 15:14).

So we see that the Christian religion is pre-eminently a religion of action. And it is as a religion of action that it best commends itself to the eyes of this cynical, doubting world. The statement of the Athenian orator, Aristides, to his emperor, is a classic in this regard. Here is what he said of the Christians of his day: "The Christians know and trust God. They placate those who oppose them and make them their friends, they do good to their enemies. Their wives are absolutely pure, and their daughters modest. Their men abstain from unlawful marriage and from all impurity. If any of them have bondwomen or children, they persuade them to become Chris-

tians, for the love they have toward them; and when they become so, they call them without distinction brothers. They
love one another. They do not refuse to help the widows. They
rescue the orphan from him who does him violence. He who
has, gives ungrudgingly to him who has not. If they see a
stranger, they take him to their dwellings and rejoice over
him as over a real brother; for they do not call themselves
brothers after the flesh, but after the spirit, and in God. If
anyone among them is poor and needy, and they do not have
food to spare, they fast for two or three days, that they may
supply him with necessary food. They scrupulously obey the
commands of their Messiah. Every morning and every hour
they thank and praise God for his loving-kindness toward
them. . . . Because of them there flows forth all the beauty that
there is in the world. But the good deeds they do they do
not proclaim in the ears of the multitude, but they take care
that no one shall perceive them. Thus they labor to become
righteous. Truly this is a new people, and there is something
divine in them."

So, in considering church membership, you must face up to
the fact that it demands a truly Christian standard of conduct. Are you willing to do what you honestly believe Jesus
would want you to do in any given situation in your life?

Are you willing to try, to the best of your ability, to love
your neighbor as yourself? That sounds easy in the general,
but it is not so easy in the specific. I never shall forget something that a fine Jewish dentist said to me. I had been going
to him for professional services for some time, and had discussed with him quite frankly many matters concerning the
religious life. He had disclosed to me that his faith in Judaism
was not strong, although he revered his Orthodox father and
spoke lovingly of him. So far as religion was concerned, he
was uncertain and inclined to be critical. I invited him to
church and presented him with a copy of the new Testament.
There were tears in his expressive eyes as he accepted it.
"Reverend," he said, "I want you to know I shall always
treasure this book. I cannot tell you how much it means to me
that you should give me a copy of your sacred Scriptures."
And then, leaning toward me, he asked: "Tell me the truth.

If I were to come to your church, would your people accept me as a brother?"

Are you willing to try to love your neighbor?

"Your neighbor" refers not only to the person who lives next door to you, but also to any person who needs your help, whether he lives next door or on the other side of the globe. See Luke 10:29-37 for Jesus' teaching in this regard. It is dynamic. "Love," said Paul, "does no wrong to a neighbor; therefore love is the fulfilling of the law" (Rom. 13:10).

Are you willing to live according to the terms of the Golden Rule? "Whatever you wish that men would do to you, do so to them" (Matt. 7:12). That word "whatever" is a big one!

Are you willing first to be reconciled to your brother?

Are you willing to turn the other cheek? To go the second mile?

Are you willing to love your enemies? To bless them that curse you? To do good to them that hate you? To pray for those who persecute you and treat you spitefully?

Are you willing to forgive? To hold your tongue when tempted to pass censorious judgment?

Are you willing to seek God's kingdom first?

All this is a part of the Christian life. It is, in fact, the principal characteristic of the true Christian life. That many nominal Christians in the church do not so live makes such living none the less necessary. Far too long have such high standards been neglected in our casual living, to the detriment of our own souls and to the confusion of the souls of others. In our modern way of thinking, the Sermon on the Mount has been pushed aside as something that cannot actually be lived out in real life. As a result, Christianity has become so tame and watered down that it will not cost anyone very much; but neither will it challenge anyone to live at his best.

What is needed in the world today is a ministry of Christian behavior so courageous that it will disturb human complacency, a faith and practice that will for once and for all take seriously the teachings of Jesus and dare to live by them. Christ's teachings are not theoretical, but vigorous and practical.

Will you be one to accept this challenge?

Cultivating Christian Attitudes

The Christian life implies action. That is true. It also implies a certain attitude. This inner attitude of the soul is absolutely essential.

Now, what is the actual inner attitude of your life? What are you really like inside? Becoming a Christian is far more than making a profession of faith with the lips, or submitting to the ordinance of baptism, or accepting a certain brand of theology. It is, we repeat, a life attitude. What is yours?

Is your life attitude one of ingrained, though possibly unsuspected, selfishness? Do all your plans, thoughts, aims, and feelings center about yourself? Do you demand a lot of attention from other people, and does your self-esteem sink to a low ebb if you do not get it? If you are on a committee, or are a member of a group in your church, Sunday school, or youth organization, do you truly wish to serve, or do you wish only to dominate? Are you pleased when someone else seems to get ahead faster than you do? Do you carry your feelings on your sleeve? Is this the attitude of a Christian? Do you not see that becoming a Christian means a change in these attitudes?

Jesus said: "If any man would come after me, let him deny himself and take up his cross daily and follow me. For whoever would save his life will lose it; but whoever loses his life for my sake, he will save it" (Luke 9:23-24). Now a word or two of explanation. This self-denial of which Jesus was speaking means more than the interpretation commonly given to it. It does not refer to denying oneself a little silver now and then for Jesus' sake. Our possessions will take their rightful place if we love him. Jesus here had reference to the denial of the clamorings of an unruly self, a self that needs to be disciplined. After all, a disciple is one who has accepted a discipline. The root of the two words, "disciple" and "discipline," is the same. And this matter of cross-bearing which Jesus mentioned means more than bearing our sorrows and our adversities bravely and uncomplainingly, although I believe that that should be our attitude toward suffering. Paul explained the matter by saying that we are to carry a cross as did Jesus, and that on that cross we are to nail the selfishness that is within us. "And those who belong to Christ Jesus," Paul avowed. "have crucified the flesh with its passions and desires" (Gal. 5:24). If we are really to follow Christ, we cannot escape feeling the weight of his cross.

This is what Jesus meant when he answered the young man who came running to him exclaiming, "What good deed must I do, to have eternal life?" It is worthy of note that this young man had a proper conception of the place of action in religion. "If you would enter into life," said Jesus, "keep the commandments." "All these I have observed," the young man replied. "What do I still lack?" Then Jesus said to him: "If you would be perfect, go, sell what you possess and give it to the poor, and you will have treasure in heaven; and come, follow me." It is written that "when the young man heard this he went away sorrowful; for he had great possessions" (Matt. 19:16-22). Jesus here was seeking to correct this young man's life attitude, to change it from one of ingrained selfishness to one of health-giving, self-discipline and service to others. But the power of his selfishness was great; it had become deeply imbedded in his personality. We are told that he weighed the price, decided against it, and went away—"sorrowful."

What a significant word! What depths of meaning are buried there! The selfish life becomes ultimately the unhappy life. To live for self means eventually to be held by the chains of self. To do just as one pleases means that at last one will not like what one pleases. But the Christian faith, if truly embraced and applied, means the ultimate release of the inner self from the chains of selfishness. This is the way of life and happiness. "Whoever would save his life," said Jesus, "will lose it." Here he meant—so I believe—"Whoever would *hoard* his life will lose it." "But," Jesus went on, "whoever loses his life for my sake and the gospel's will save it." In other words, if we give ourselves to him, he will give us back ourselves, redeemed and liberated.

"What makes a man a Christian," declared Dr. John Baille of the University of Edinburgh, "is neither his intellectual acceptance of certain ideas, nor his conformity to a certain rule, but his possession of a certain spirit and his participation in a certain life."

We live in a world that suffers from a vast neurosis, a world that has been attacked by a mass psychology of selfishness which is the very opposite of the Christian faith. We are immersed in it every day of our lives. It is the spirit of our times. If man is to find himself, this spirit of selfishness which lies at the root of all our misery must give place to the higher spirit of the Christian faith. To join the church means to build in oneself an attitude toward life that is Christian, even though the church itself may be caught at times in the downward pull of this great sickness of the soul.

This is not to say that one is to hate himself or can expect to free himself entirely from self-interest. That would be impossible. Jesus does not ask us to assume so unnatural a role in life. Self-respect and personal dignity are essential. He said, "You shall love your neighbor as yourself." However, he had first said, "You shall love your God with all your heart." He meant, I think, that one should ennoble and purify self-love and put it in its proper place by embracing the highest love of all, the love of God. Thus the emphasis is placed, not on self, but on God and on others. If one would love himself as he ought, let him first love others as he ought.

All this is in the Christian faith. There is no conversion without it, for conversion is essentially a change from a self-centered existence to a Christ-centered life. For the Christian, the center is no longer self; it is Christ. He is the Lord of life. He is the Master of the soul.

Are you willing that your life shall have this new center? Are you willing that the dominant voice shall pass from self to Christ? Think about this carefully. Comprehend its implications, and then act.

Developing a Christian Philosophy

What is your philosophy of life? By "philosophy" I mean world-view. What is your world-view? Do you believe there is a God? If so, in what kind of God do you believe? Do you believe the universe has purpose and aim in it? Do you believe it is going somewhere? Do you believe God governs in the affairs of men?

You are formulating your life-philosophy. What direction is it taking? You had better find out! You had better take it in hand, examine it closely, and make it Christian before someone else directs it in a way that is not Christian.

For, frankly, there are forces about you that would make your life-philosophy materialistic and mechanistic. That is, they would teach you that in the last analysis you came into existence by blind chance, by a "fortuitous concourse of circumstances," and that you and all mankind are headed for extinction. They would tell you that there is no meaning to life, no divine point of reference, no soul in the scheme of things; they would have you believe that the universe is racing toward destruction, like an express train roaring through the night with a dead engineer in the cab. Or they would tell you that the universe is slowly running down like a great clock, and will sometime hang motionless and mute in the vast cold of interplanetary space.

Not much room for God in a system like that! Not much hope either! For if I am going it all alone in the universe, with no divine point of reference, no God to care, then my work has little meaning, and my life is truly tragic. Modern man is now suffering from a sense of cosmic loneliness. Recently an honor student in one of our great universities, unable to formulate an adequate philosophy of life, dejectedly wrote these forlorn words to a friend: "Here on this whirling globe, a mere speck of congealed mud on the fringe of the solar system, the worms, you and I, live, aspire, strive, and die. Where is the meaning of life? Is there really any? Again and again I find myself face to face with this question. Like a butterfly against a window, I seem to beat aimlessly. I suppose that my impotency and my utter blankness in the face of eternal enigma is one reason for the fits of utter depression into which I fall at times."

What a sorry confession! Yet it is the natural outcome of a philosophy which sees in life no meaning and no purpose, no God and no soul. Try as he may, man cannot escape the fact which Augustine had in mind when he prayed to God: "Thou has made us for thyself, and our souls are restless until they rest in thee." To live adequately, one must have an adequate philosophy of life. There must be at the center of one's thinking a place for God.

The Christian philosophy of life affirms that both the universe and man have come from the hand of God. It affirms also that everything God made was good. When you read the first two chapters of Genesis, do so with this thought in mind and you will not become confused. The Christian philosophy of life holds that the destiny of the universe is redemption. The world is to be purified and will behold the coming of the kingdom of heaven. "The kingdom of the world," announce the voices of Revelation, "has become the kingdom of our Lord and of his Christ" (Rev. 11:15).

There is purpose and aim in the course of human events. It may not seem so on the surface, but it is true nevertheless. The providence of God may be likened to an ocean liner. Each of its parts, if alone, would sink, but when each part is related to the others, then it floats and it can go somewhere. There is an upward trend in the affairs of men. Each of us has a part to perform in bringing about the ultimate, glorious, eternal destiny of the world. Jesus taught his disciples to pray:

> "Thy kingdom come,
> Thy will be done,
> On earth as it is in heaven."

Jesus would not ask us to offer a prayer that would be forever hopeless.

We are not alone. The Great Companion promised he would never leave or forsake us. We live in the hollow of his hand, and no man shall ever pluck us out of it. If you would know what God is like, look at Jesus Christ. He is the full and complete revelation of the Father. "He who has seen me," he quietly said to Philip, "has seen the Father. . . . I and the Father are one" (John 14:9; 10:30). If you would know the heart of God, read Luke's Gospel, chapter fifteen. You will find there that God is like a good shepherd, like a watchful housewife, and like a father, eternally seeking the lost.

You will have a master. That is inevitable. Someone, something, will master you. Who, what, shall it be?

Will it be love of money? Love of money, which only increases man's anxiety and uneasiness?

Will it be love of pleasure? Love of pleasure, which never brings its devotee true happiness?

Will it be love of power? Love of power, which only corrupts the human soul?

Will it be love of God through Jesus Christ? Will you give the whole allegiance of your life to Jesus? He is to be the Master as well as the Savior of your life. His name is Lord and Master. Lord, grant it may be so. For through him you will come to peace, you will be made adequate; you will find life. Just now, in the quiet of your thoughts, whisper this prayer, "Lord Jesus, take all of me there is."

QUESTIONS FOR DISCUSSION

1. After reading this chapter and in light of your own experience, what does it mean to accept Jesus Christ as your Savior? As your Lord?

2. What was your conversion experience? Was it different from what you expected it to be?

3. What is faith? What is its relationship to salvation?

4. How far should one go in the matter of public confession of specific sins? Explain your answer. Why is confession of sin to God necessary for salvation?

5. What is salvation? What is its relationship to this life? To the life to come?

PROJECTS AND REPORTS

1. Ask representative members of your church, including the deacons and other officials, how they were converted, and what they believe the Christian life to be. Give a résumé of your findings to the class.

2. Find out how your church receives new members. What methods of preparing converts for church membership are employed? Report your findings to the class.

CHAPTER II

The Nature and Mission of the Church

The Church: Its Origin

The church is different from all other institutions on earth in that it was established by Jesus Christ. No other explanation can account for its presence in the world. That it has endured and prospered throughout the centuries despite the human, erring element in it is eloquent testimony to the fact that it came from a divine source. "I will build my church," Jesus said firmly, "and the powers of death shall not prevail against it" (Matt. 16:18). It is an institution which Jesus loved and for which he gave himself. "Christ loved the church," Paul explains, "and gave himself up for her, that he might consecrate her" (Eph. 5:25-26). Furthermore, Jesus Christ himself is the Head of the church. "He is the head of the body, the church," Paul states; "he is the beginning, the first-born from the dead, that in everything he might be preëminent" (Col. 1:18).

From that divine origin the church has come down to us through the years. It is a sacred heritage. Consecrated people of other generations, other races, other tongues, and other nationalities have handed it down to us. The church is here today, still performing its ministry of redemption because people of other days loved it enough to identify themselves with it, to support it with their prayers and sacrificial gifts, to live the life it exemplified, and even to die for it when it became necessary. God grant that we who follow in their train may be worthy of them!

According to New Testament teaching and example, the church is a body of baptized believers. That is to say, it is made up of persons who have openly professed their faith in God through Jesus Christ by baptism, and thus have entered the fellowship of the believers. "Just as the body is one and has many members," Paul affirms, "and all the members of the body, though many are one body, so it is with Christ.

20

For by one Spirit we were all baptized into one body—Jews or Greeks, slaves or free—and all were made to drink of one Spirit" (1 Cor. 12:12-13).

Thus we perceive that this institution which Jesus founded is a closely knit fellowship, a fellowship so intimate and interdependent that it is called a body. As a body, its various members have certain vital, indispensable duties to perform, and without the faithful performance of any one of these duties the entire body suffers. In this fellowship, artificial distinctions of race, color, nationality, creed, and social status disappear, and all are one. This oneness is made possible through obedience to the Head of the body, which is Jesus Christ.

The Church: A Fellowship with a Mission

1. *Primarily, then, the church is a fellowship whose responsibility is that of love.* It is a *koinonia*, that is to say, a "fellowship." *Koinonia* is the New Testament Greek term, and it is often used by writers to describe the spirit that existed in that first-century fellowship of believers. It is the term used by Luke when he affirms; "They devoted themselves to the apostles' teaching and fellowship, to the breaking of bread and the prayers" (Acts 2:42). In the same spirit Peter wrote, "Having purified your souls by your obedience to the truth for a sincere love of the brethren, love one another earnestly from the heart" (1 Pet. 1:22). These references indicate the horizontal aspect of fellowship; that is, fellowship with the brethren. But Paul uses the term *koinonia* to express also the vertical aspect of fellowship; that is, fellowship with Christ. "God is faithful," he says, "by whom you were called into the fellowship of his Son, Jesus Christ our Lord" (1 Cor. 1:9). John also writes: "That which we have seen and heard we proclaim also to you, so that you may have fellowship with us; and our fellowship is with the Father and with his Son Jesus Christ" (1 John 1:3).

Hence, we see that the church is a body of people united in a fellowship that is both human and divine. It is a fellowship made possible through the Father himself. It is not so much a fellowship *of* the Spirit as it is a fellowship *in* the Spirit. The *koinonia* is both the divine Presence that unites the body and the body that is united. It is a fellowship of that which is shared and of those who share it.

2. *The church is a distinctive fellowship.* It is a body of people who are united in a fellowship that lives, thinks, and moves on a high plane. The church is also the *ekkleisia;* that is, the "called-out ones." That is the term Jesus used when he said, "On this rock I will build my church" (Matt. 16:18). The church, then, is a fellowship of those who have pledged themselves to live on a moral plane that lies above the plane of the world about them. This they have pledged themselves to do, not in vain self-righteousness, but in deep humility. They have accepted a discipline. This thought is challengingly expressed by Paul when he writes:

> "Therefore come out from them,
> and be separate from them, says the Lord,
> and touch nothing unclean;
> then I will welcome you."—*2 Corinthians 6:17*

James echoes this idea in the words: "Religion that is pure and undefiled before God and the Father is this: to visit orphans and widows in their affliction, and to keep oneself unstained from the world" (James 1:27).

3. *Even so, the church is also an imperfect fellowship.* It must be; otherwise none could ever qualify for membership in it. This is said, not that we may presume upon or abuse the privilege of membership, but that all may take hope. It must have been a fellowship of the imperfect in those first-century days, or Paul would never have said to the Corinthian church: "While there is jealousy and strife among you, are you not of the flesh, and behaving like ordinary men?" (1 Cor. 3:3).

What Dr. Charles Clayton Morrison has stated is therefore true: "The Christian church is not a society of integrated personalities, nor of philosophers, nor of mystics, nor even of good people. It is a society of broken personalities, of men and women with troubled minds, of people who know that they are not good." [1] Dr. Elton Trueblood adds: "Those who make

[1] Charles Clayton Morrison, in *What Is Christianity?* Copyright, 1940, by Harper and Brothers. Used by permission.

up the nameless order are not united by their virtue, for they are not virtuous; neither are they united by their superior intelligence or piety. Their only bond of union is their *concern.*" [2] What is significant, however, and certainly not a fact to be overlooked, is that these individuals have frankly acknowledged their sins and shortcomings, and by uniting with the church have declared their intention to live, with Christ's help, a nobler life.

4. *The church is a democratic fellowship.* In obedience to Jesus' wish, there were to be no "masters" in it. "Neither be called masters," he warned them, "for you have one master, the Christ. He who is greatest among you shall be your servant; whoever exalts himself shall be humbled" (Matt. 23: 10-12).

In the New Testament churches there were only two kinds of church officers—pastors and deacons. Their qualifications are set forth in 1 Timothy, chapter 3. The word "bishop," in the original Greek, is *episkopos,* which means literally "pastor." So Paul is saying in effect: "If anyone aspires to the office of pastor he desires a noble task" (1 Tim. 3:1). However, these officials were chosen not to rule arbitrarily over the flock, but to guide them, counsel them, pray for them, and assist them in every way possible. The pastors were to exercise spiritual oversight over the congregation. The deacons were to see that the material needs of the members were cared for. In all matters, the church as a whole had the deciding voice.

Luke, in the sixth chapter of Acts, tells us this: "Now in these days when the disciples were increasing in number, the Hellenists murmured against the Hebrews because their widows were neglected in the daily distribution. And the twelve summoned the body of the disciples and said, 'It is not right that we should give up preaching the word of God to serve tables. Therefore, brethren, pick out from among you seven men of good repute, full of the Spirit and of wisdom, whom we may appoint to this duty. But we will devote ourselves to prayer and to the ministry of the word'" (Acts 6:1-4). It is important to note that the deacons in the first-century church were

[2] Elton Trueblood, in *Alternative to Futility.* Copyright, 1948, by Harper and Brothers. Used by permission.

chosen by the members as a whole, not appointed by the apostles. Generally speaking, the duties of the pastors were prayer and the ministry of the Word, and the duties of the deacons concerned the daily distribution to the widows and other needy persons in the fellowship. At times, however, the deacons performed a spiritual ministry as well.

The democratic nature of this fellowship is further indicated by the manner in which the early church undertook the responsibility to help other churches, and also in the manner in which they arrived at decisions in church policy. When in days of famine a call for help came to the Antioch church, it was the church as a group that decided to send relief to the brethren living at Jerusalem. This obligation was not placed upon the church by any higher ecclesiastical authority (Acts 11:27-30). When the dispute arose in the Christian community as to whether circumcision should be demanded of Gentile converts to the Christian faith, it was the church in session that made the decision, not the leaders or officials. Church leaders voiced their opinion, but the decision was made by the church (Acts 15). The church is a democratic fellowship.

5. *The church is an inspired fellowship.* The church is a fellowship with a mission. It is a startling and noteworthy fact that Jesus took ordinary people, filled them with a sense of mission, and said to them, "You are the salt of the earth. . . . You are the light of the world. A city set on a hill cannot be hid" (Matt. 5:13-14). His words have this force: "You are a distinctive fellowship; you are to redeem and preserve society. You are to do the work of God!" He said to them, "As the Father has sent me, even so I send you" (John 20:21).

The disciples were so thrilled with this sense of divine destiny and partnership with Christ that they literally were transformed and freed from fear. They dared to defy even the power of the Sanhedrin. It is said of the Jewish authorities that "when they saw the boldness of Peter and John, and perceived that they were uneducated, common men, they wondered; and they recognized that they had been with Jesus" (Acts 4:13).

The disciples were charged with the task of evangelizing the world. Inspired with that urgent sense of mission, they "turned the world upside down" (Acts 17:6).

6. *The church is a concerned fellowship.* That is to say, the early Christians were a society of people who cared, who cared for the world and for one another.

"And all who believed," states Luke, "were together and had all things in common" (Acts 2:44). They prayed for one another. "Is any among you sick?" asks James. "Let him call for the elders of the church, and let them pray over him. . . . Pray one for another, that you may be healed" (James 5:14-16). They watched over one another in a helpful, Christlike way. "Brethren," Paul admonishes, "if a man is overtaken in any trespass, you who are spiritual should restore him in a spirit of gentleness. . . . Bear one another's burdens, and so fulfill the law of Christ" (Gal. 6:1-2). James echoes this noble thought when he says: "My brethren, if any one among you wanders from the truth and some one brings him back, let him know that whoever brings back a sinner from the error of his way will save his soul from death and will cover a multitude of sins" (James 5:19-20).

7. *The church is a dynamic fellowship.* The church was, and ever should be, a fellowship that imparts to its members a purpose to live *for* and a power to live *by*. Fellowship such as has been described is dynamic. The members of it have the encouragement which comes from belonging to an interested and concerned group. They know that they are not alone. This knowledge also is a dynamic. Changes take place when one joins oneself to the group, and the changes invariably are toward higher and better things.

It has been said that the early Christians conquered the old pagan, Roman world and its superstitions because they outlived and outdied the pagans. I believe that this was true. I believe also that they outlived and outdied their adversaries because of the courage they received from the Christian fellowship of the church. Their sense of God was powerful, and their faith in Christ was vital. Thus, they were undergirded for the times when they had to endure fiery trials. They were better able to endure their sufferings because they knew that at that very moment a little band of believers was meeting and praying for them. For an illustration of this, see Acts, chapter 12.

This continues to be one of the finest services that the church can render. I can still remember the significant statement one of our young men once made when, in a small, informal gathering, an opportunity was given for the expression of some personal impressions and experiences. George had not been with us very long. Having come from a rural community to a large city, he had not found it easy to adjust his life to that of the church group. But due to the infectious, Christian enthusiasm of our young people, he had been led out and up. He was beginning to see for the first time, so it seemed, what a cohesive Christian community really meant to one's life. He was feeling the saving impact of Christian influence. He was beginning to understand how much fun a *good* time could be. All this was coming to a climax in his own soul as he stood up that evening in our church and uttered one simple sentence, "Now I know the kind of life I want."

Few things encourage the Christian more or give greater impetus to his convictions than fellowship with other Christian people. No other institution provides such a frankly Christian atmosphere. In that sense, every youth group or adult group, and every church service or social occasion, becomes a channel of healing friendliness. A lone atom is a meaningless atom. When a lone individual gravitates toward a church and there finds a true fellowship, he soon begins to know the kind of life he wants. What is even more important, he becomes able to live it!

Dr. Charles T. Holman has declared: "There is nothing the threatened soul needs more than the sustaining power of a warm and loyal fellowship. The sense of isolation is a prolific cause of personality disorder. A friend of mine who became psychological consultant in a gastrointestinal clinic discovered that one of his first needs in caring for his patients was to discover groups into which they might be introduced and where they could find real friendship. They needed, for recovery to health, to be received into some group in which they would be valued, respected, and loved, and where they would be given opportunity to participate in activities directed toward worth-while ends. They needed to be saturated with the spirit of groups which cherished wholesome attitudes of faith, hope, love and self-respect. And these groups he found first of all in the churches." [3]

Now, the church is able to provide such a dynamic, not only because it has fellowship to offer, but also because it has worship to offer. Worship is yet another dynamic.

"This world can be saved from political chaos and collapse," said the Archbishop of Canterbury recently, "by one thing only, and that is worship." I know that sounds much like a preacher talking, a preacher who just wants people to come to church, but let us listen while the Archbishop explains worship. "To worship is to quicken the conscience by the holiness of God, to feed the mind with the truth of God, to purge the imagination by the beauty of God, and to devote the will to the purpose of God."

The world needs desperately to be saved. It needs to be saved economically, politically, socially, and personally, but it will not be so saved until it is first saved spiritually. It will not be saved spiritually until its people return to God's house, where the lost splendor of life may be recaptured, where conscience may become sensitized, where motives may be revealed and purified, where vision may be clarified, where man may look up from the present and see the eternal, where he may look beyond the visible and approach Him who is invisible, where he may be lifted out of the limitations of the present and enter the broad scope of God's eternal, unfailing purposes, where he may receive assurance that God governs in the affairs of men and that man does not walk alone!

When one has experienced this in worship, he is prepared to live. Scientists today have stepped into the pulpit, as it were, and are proclaiming that the world will not be saved until people find their way back to God. They insist that a spiritual recovery must come. However, the spiritual recovery will not come, and people will not find their way back to God, until they come back to worship.

In addition, the church is able to provide such a dynamic because it offers opportunities for service, and service is still another dynamic. Service meets a fundamental need in human

[3] Charles Holman, in *Getting Down to Cases*. Copyright, 1942, The Macmillan Co. Used by permission.

personality. To be competent, one's life must be a channel
instead of a reservoir, a river Jordan instead of a Dead Sea.
One must learn to be and to do, instead of only to have and to
get. The life that is centered about the self goes to pieces. The
life that is centered about a worthy cause and is given in
worthy service is the life that finds itself and produces a well-
rounded personality. It is precisely this type of outgoing service
that the church offers to anyone who will take advantage of it.

Modern psychologists, men of science who know the human
personality, are telling their patients to go to church, to join
the church, and to go to work in the church, if they would
achieve the best in mental health. "The greatest discovery in
modern education," affirmed Prof. W. H. Kilpatrick, "is that
he who saves his life shall lose it. He that loses his life in a
great cause shall find it."

The church provides opportunity for service, self-expression,
and contribution that builds character, enlarges personality,
and develops talent.

Young men and women have been literally drawn out of
themselves and transformed by the simple act of making oc-
casional short talks in youth meetings. Adults have been able
to forget themselves and their sorrows by taking responsibility
for classes of boys or girls, and by working with them and for
them on the Lord's Day and during the week. Shy persons
have developed into able church leaders because they consented
to assume some sort of responsibility in a youth organization.
High school boys and girls have been inspired through service
in the church to become ministers and missionaries. The church
is the finest training ground for personality development.

I think I became a minister partly because when I was a high
school student I had a pastor who took an interest in the
youth of his church. He asked me to have a part at various
times in the evening church service. He asked me to lead the
Sunday school singing. This meant much for me. I was a
timid farm boy and was so self-conscious that I was afraid
of my own voice. It struck actual terror to my heart when
I was asked to do anything in a public way. I believe I got
my start in personality, character, and vocational development
in my home church.

This fellowship in service is dynamic, not only for character, personality, and the soul, but also for talent. Many of our finest musicians received their first inspiration to follow music professionally in a church choir. It was in religious singing groups that their talent was discovered, encouraged, and developed.

Grace Moore had her first taste of music in a church choir. However, it was the church, rather than music, that attracted her. Marian Anderson sang in her church when she was only eight years of age. When she became a little older, she substituted for regular singers in the church choir if they were absent. When she had grown up, she was admitted to the regular choir. She says, "My choir work is partly responsible for my sound musicianship." How infinitely poorer the world of music would be today were it not for the church!

These opportunities, and scores of similar ones, are available to all.

8. *The church is a redemptive fellowship.* It is more than a fellowship with a mission; it is a fellowship with a commission; i.e., the Great Commission! "Go therefore," commanded Jesus, "and make dsciples of all nations." The early disciples were thrilled by the challenge to evangelize the world. They saw the world as in the bondage of destruction. They saw mankind as hopelessly lost without Christ. They had the answer. They had Christ, who possessed the power of an endless life. They were to make disciples, baptize them, and teach them the will of Jesus Christ. They had more than a way of life to proclaim; they had the Life!

This is the church's peculiar prerogative and privilege. Its task is—first, last, and always—to redeem mankind. This the church has been doing from that day to this. As the ancient writer exclaimed, "From them has come everything that is good in this world." Influences stream out from the church that reach into every home in the nation and throughout the world.

This is the kind of organization you are joining. Your church is an evangelistic, missionary fellowship. It is but one of the thousands of churches of every denomination which are supporting Christian teachers, nurses, doctors, agriculturists, and many other types of worth-while missionary service in every corner of the globe. The churches' missionaries are on the teeming streets of the great cities. They are in isolated settlements. They are in America. They are abroad. Your church is in business, important business, all over the world.

An American airman is shot down at sea. He paddles his lifeboat toward an unknown and possibly hostile shore. He is behind enemy lines. He has been told there may be cannibals on this island. As he draws near he sees, awaiting him, giant-sized black men on the beach. But he is not eaten or tortured. Instead, he is carefully nursed back to health, hidden from the enemy, and safely transported to the nearest American base. The missionaries had been there before him. They had tamed and transformed raw, unadulterated savages, often at the cost of their own lives. These wild, ebony-skinned creatures had been redeemed from superstition and murder by the gospel of Jesus Christ, preached to them by Christian missionaries, who had been sent out by the Christian churches of America.

An Associated Press correspondent bailed out over the jungles of New Guinea. When he finally found his way to a native village, his first question to bring a satisfactory response was, "Where missionary station?" Later he wrote: "Many churchgoers had seemed hypocrites to me, but watching those two underfed missionaries, who had risked their lives to stay with the natives in the jungle, noting the quiet joy on their faces as they worked and worshiped, I realized I must have been wrong." [4]

Obscene worship was destroying the people of Hawaii. There had not been that idyllic effect of native paganism that the skeptic is so fond of mouthing. The people were poverty-stricken and terror-ridden when the first missionaries came to them early in the nineteenth century. The seventeen missionaries and workers who came were not wild-eyed, long-haired, jaundiced fanatics who thumped improvised pulpits in the jungle and waved limp Bibles. They were sane, trained, practical-minded individuals. There were two ministers, a printer, a doctor, a farmer, teachers, and other helpers. Their assignment was overwhelming. They were to give the people

[4] Based on facts presented in *They Found the Church There*, by Henry P. Van Dusen. Copyright, 1945, Charles Scribner's Sons.

churches, schools, agriculture, homes, the Bible, and Christ. They were to teach the natives to read and write. This tremendous order was filled! In twenty-six years 80 per cent of the population could read and write. This unbelievable task was accomplished at the cost of only one million dollars.[5] The church is a redemptive fellowship.

9. *The church is a preserving fellowship.* The church stands today a silent sentinel over the rights, liberties, and morals of the people. No other institution exerts such far-reaching influence. To the superficial observer it may appear archaic and ineffective, but there is no way of knowing just how far its preserving and correcting influence has sunk into the unconscious mind of the world. Suffice it to say that the church could not be uprooted without pulling its tendrils out of the very heart of every phase of our culture.

This fact was dramatically illustrated during World War II. In 1933 Hitler boasted, "I promise you if I wish to I could destroy the church in a few years. It is hollow, false, and rotten through and through." The words of Albert Einstein are now familiar: "When National Socialism came to Germany I looked to the universities to defend freedom, knowing they had always boasted of their devotion to the truth. They were immediately silenced. Then I looked to the great editors of the newspapers whose flaming editorials had proclaimed love of freedom. They were silenced in a few short weeks. I looked to the individual writers who had written much of the place of freedom in modern life. They, too, were mute. Only the churches stood squarely across Hitler's campaign to suppress truth. I never had special interest in the church before, but now I feel a great affection and admiration, because the church alone had the courage and persistence to stand for intellectual truth and moral freedom. I am forced thus to confess that what I once despised I now praise unreservedly."

During those terrible days of war in Europe, it was the Christian church that stood firmly for the right of church and school to preach and teach the truth. It was the Christian church that defended the Jews and withstood corrupt political leadership.

---

[5] Based on facts presented in *On Our Own Doorstep*, by Frank S. Mead. Copyright, 1948, The Friendship Press.

It was the Christian church that denounced the execution of the aged and insane, and sought to preserve the youth of the land. It was the Christian church that, at the price of blood and sacrifice, championed human rights.

10. *The church is a unifying fellowship.* I know that the charge is often made that Christianity has a divisive influence. This divisiveness is more apparent than real. When the Nazis struck in Germany, all the Christian forces joined hands, regardless of creed and polity. Indeed, the faith of the Christian churches provides the world with its one basis of unity. The world cannot be united on the basis of color, because there are many different colors. It cannot be united on the basis of social or economic status, for that will always be a variable. The world cannot be united on the basis of patriotism, for that, too, is a divisive element. But it can be united on the basis of Christian faith and practice, for these are universal in their adaptability. When World War II ended, Christians all over the globe, Christians of many races and nationalities, were praying for each other, even for their brethren in enemy lands. This is the true Christian community.

"Why don't the churches get together?" someone asks. "Why do there have to be so many different churches?" I recognize the fact that sometimes loyalty to the Christian life becomes but little more than loyalty to a certain brand of religion. Sometimes the churches do become divisive in their influence. However, denominational differences are the price of religious freedom. If one is to grant to a people the right to worship God as they see fit, then one must allow for differences in interpretation of the Scriptures and of the will of God. These differences of interpretation and opinion are the basis of the denominationalism that exists today. The alternative would be a religious dictatorship. Those who know church history recognize how pernicious such a dictatorship can be. If we are to have religious freedom, it seems we must also have denominationalism.

However, denominationalism does not prevent spiritual unity and co-operation. Such unity and co-operation are the will of Jesus Christ and the burden of his priestly prayer: "I have manifested thy name to the men whom thou gavest me out of the world; thine they were, and thou gavest them to me. . . . I do not pray for these only, but also for those who are to believe in me through their word, that they may all be one; even as thou, Father, art in me, and I in thee, that they also may be in us, so that the world may believe that thou hast sent me. The glory which thou hast given me I have given to them, that they may be one even as we are one, I in them and thou in me, that they may become perfectly one, so that the world may know that thou hast sent me and hast loved them even as thou hast loved me" (John 17:6, 20-23).

QUESTIONS FOR DISCUSSION

1. What would be an ideal church? To what extent does your church meet the ideal for the church as expressed in this chapter? Is it possible for a church to achieve such an ideal?

2. What does the term "fellowship" mean to you? What is your church doing to realize this ideal of fellowship? What is your church doing to draw others into this fellowship? What in the life of your church was instrumental in drawing you into its fellowship?

3. What terms are used in the Scriptures to describe the church? What is the significance of each?

PROJECTS AND REPORTS

1. Ask representative citizens of your community—a doctor, a lawyer, an undertaker, a salesman, a merchant, the mayor, etc.—what they honestly think of the church. If they belong to a church, why did they join it? If they do not, why have they not?

2. Find out what means are being employed in your community to promote spiritual unity among the churches.

CHAPTER III

You Are Responsible

What Are the Responsibilities?

You are uniting with a church, the body of Christ and the object of his love. You are uniting with it because there is a need in your soul for the message and the inspiration of the church. There is something noble in it that you want for yourself. But you are also uniting with it because there is something you wish to give and to do. Christ's work is unfinished. This unfinished work is for us to do. He is depending on us. You are uniting with a church, then, because you wish to accept a responsibility, a sacred responsibility to do your part for your Master and for your fellow man. You wish to have a part in forwarding the noble ministry of the church. You wish to affiliate yourself with that inspired army of men and women of past ages who have felt this same holy responsibility, joined the church, forwarded its work, and made it possible for you in the twentieth century to hear the gospel and know the Christ.

Specifically, then, what are these responsibilities? What are the ways in which you may co-operate with Jesus and thus forward his kingdom through the church which you are joining?

Serving

First of all, there is the responsibility to serve. The church carries on its work very largely because there are men and women, young people and children, who are willing to give without remuneration their time and talent in places of service. The pastor's work is indispensable to the life of the church, but he would be relatively helpless without the consistent and unselfish help of Christians who teach Sunday church school classes, visit the sick, do visitation evangelism, lead youth groups, work with children's organizations, lead men's fellowships or women's societies, sing in the choir, or work on the financial committees. Consider how poor and ineffective the church would be without the church workers I have mentioned above, and I have given only a partial list.

Somewhere in the church you are joining, there is a place of service awaiting you. It may not appear to you now what it can possibly be, but it is there. God has given you a talent to be used somewhere in his work. You will be held accountable if you neglect that talent or use it wrongly. It may be you have a voice you can give to the Lord by singing in the church choir. How many people have been inspired to higher levels of living by the human voice lifted in song in divine service, no one will ever know. Perhaps you have a place of service waiting for you in the Youth Fellowship, in one of the adult organizations, or on one of the Boards of the church. Whatever it is and wherever it is, hold yourself ready to serve, for this is a part of your responsibility.

Of all the work that is done in and by the church, the work of the Sunday church school teacher is probably the most far-reaching and determinative so far as life-influences are concerned. I shall never forget a teacher I had when I was in the Primary Department. She wielded an influence over me greater than my day-school teacher. Her face was kind and smiling, and as she taught us Sunday by Sunday I had the feeling that she was a kind of angel hovering over us. I know that something of the sweetness of her soul found its way into mine. No finer opportunity for soul-winning and character-building can be found than that which is possessed by a Sunday church school teacher. Should an opportunity come to you to help carry on this sacred work, you should accept the responsibility.

Learning

However, along with this responsibility of service comes the equally important obligation of learning. It is not enough to be willing to serve; one must also be willing to learn how to serve to the best of one's ability. Of course, it is true that one learns by doing, and that if one waited to serve until he was perfectly prepared, he never would serve. Nevertheless, if you wish to be successful in teaching a Sunday school class, you should know something of the teachings of the Bible, the beliefs and practices of your church, the proper methods of instruction, and the personal characteristics of the age group you expect to teach.

Anyone who helps others learn must first develop a growing faith and be able to articulate it. Prior to taking on the responsibility of teaching, as well as while teaching, biblical study and other personal growth opportunities are essential. Participating in Bible study groups already existing in one's church is one good way to come to a more full understanding of the biblical message.

The following resources for leader development are available: Theological perspective books are prepared for the Christian Faith and Work Curriculum Plan with companion study guide. Study of these books helps teachers examine their personal theological perspective concerning the key issues of the curriculum. Guidance in methods is available in "Focus on the Teaching Ministry." Many books are available on understanding the needs of an age group and the principles of teaching.

For additional help, contact your state or regional director of Christian education, who is located at the American Baptist office in your state or region. Or write direct to Leader Development, American Baptist Board of Education and Publication, Valley Forge, Pennsylvania 19481.

In addition, you will want to form the habit of daily Bible study. "Do your best to present yourself to God as one approved," Paul advised, "a workman who has no need to be ashamed, rightly handling the word of truth" (2 Tim. 2:15). Do not try to read for distance. Try to read for profit. Sometimes more benefit is realized from reading and thinking on one short passage of Scripture than from a quick skimming of two or three chapters. Set aside for yourself a "quiet hour" of study, prayer, and meditation. It may be at the beginning of the day, it may be at its close, or it may be at both times. But be consistent and regular in your time of prayer and meditation.

A Japanese girl of Buddhist background had asked permission to use one of the pianos in our church for practice during the week. We invited her to the church services. She responded and became interested in the Christian life. Finally she said,

"I want to become a Christian, and to be a member of your church; but first I want to know what is required and what your beliefs are." Consequently I arranged to meet with her for several Saturday mornings for private instruction. At our first conference I said, "I want you first of all to buy a New Testament. Get the Revised Standard Version. It is written in modern English, and you can understand it more easily than the King James Version. I want you to read and study it each day, in the morning and in the evening." She did so. Each Saturday that we met, she came with her questions, and I could see that she was growing in her understanding of the Christian life. "Now," she confided to me one day, "I feel I really know what they are talking about in the Sunday school class." Then I felt she was ready to be baptized. Quietly and sincerely she made her public profession of faith in Christ and was baptized into the fellowship of our church.

One has the responsibility to learn. This opportunity is provided by our churches, and not in the Sunday church school only, but also in pastor's classes and courses in leadership education. Avail yourself of every opportunity to learn, in order that you may be better able to serve. The returns are many and infinitely worth while.

Giving

You have the responsibility also to give of your means. You should give to the best of your ability, for giving is a sacred means provided by the church whereby you may have part in the preaching of the gospel in your own community, in promoting city mission work, in maintaining missionary teachers, doctors, and workers on the foreign field, and in enabling your church to have in many other ways a saving outreach. You may not be called to preach the gospel, but you can help train someone else to do so. You may not be called to go to China as a missionary, but you can help send someone else. You may not find it possible to go to Burma to help rebuild destroyed missionary compounds and schools, but you can help send someone who can go. All this is a part of the Lord's work and you can do it.

Your church depends for its existence and service on the giving of its members. You will be expected to do your part. You will not be expected to do above that which you are able, but you will be expected to do your fair share. Your church probably has a system of taking annual pledges for the support of its work in your community (current expenses), and for the support of the work done for Christ by your denomination elsewhere in our country and in foreign lands (benevolences). You should sign such a pledge card upon becoming a member of the church, and consider contributing as your church suggests.

A Christian should give freely and cheerfully. A gift of money made grudgingly and unwillingly is not acceptable to God. "Each one must do as he has made up his mind," Paul counseled, "not reluctantly or under compulsion, for God loves a cheerful giver" (2 Cor. 9:7). Someone once said, "Give until it hurts." Someone else, correcting that statement, said, "Give until it quits hurting."

A Christian should not give with any thought of reward. In true giving the thought of receiving benefit thereby is not present. God does bless the cheerful and liberal giver, and many a Christian has testified that through the right kind of giving his personal affairs have prospered; yet that thought should not be uppermost in a person's mind when he gives. He is to give without consideration for any possible return.

A man should first give himself before making his gift. In telling the Corinthians of the liberality of the Macedonian Christians, Paul said: "First they gave themselves to the Lord and to us by the will of God" (2 Cor. 8:5).

Giving should be systematic and proportionate. Following the superb Resurrection Chapter, Paul wrote: "On the first day of every week, each of you is to put something aside and save, as he may prosper, so that contributions need not be made when I come" (1 Cor. 16:2). Paul refers here to a missionary collection for the needy brethren of Jerusalem, but the method is the point of attention. "On the first day of every week," he says. That is systematic giving. "As he may prosper," he says. That is proportionate giving. "Just what is proportionate giving?" you may ask. "What basis shall I use to determine my fair share?" These are natural questions and deserve an answer.

One Christian group, in seeking such an answer, adopted the following program of action:

1. We shall try to grow spiritually each day by having some sort of private devotion.

2. We shall strive to win someone else to Christ within the year.

3. We shall give one-tenth (the tithe) of our income to the work of Christ.

4. We shall be loyal to all the services of our church and support them with our presence unless it is utterly impossible for us to do so.

Are not these noble ideals? And at the heart of them is *tithing*, the giving of one-tenth of one's income to the work of the church.

"But," someone objects, "I give what I can spare. That is all I can do." That is not systematic giving, and giving that is not systematic usually ends up as less than what one spends for movies during the week. Giving to be adequate must be systematic and proportionate. Someone else says, "I give a tithe. I give one-tenth of what I have left when all my expenses are paid." That is not tithing. On that basis the Lord would receive very little. Another states, "I tithe, but I divide it among the social and welfare agencies of the community, and my lodge dues also come out of it." Again that is not tithing, for in scriptural tithing the tithe is brought to the Lord's house and is placed upon the altar for the Lord's work.

The best recommendation I can make to you as you start out upon the Christian life and church membership is that you adopt a systematic and proportionate method of giving, and that you consider the tithe as a proper basis for proportionate giving.

You will be helped in developing an approach to Christian giving if you will think about the basic principle of stewardship—that everything we are and have comes from God and should be used for the fulfillment of his purposes. William J. Keech has expressed it this way:

The Christian idea of stewardship is based primarily on belief in a sovereign God who created and directs the universe he made for his own self-appointed ends. He owns and controls his universe. He created man, endowed him, and made him a free agent in order that man might voluntarily work with God. God's providence is evident in the abundant and adequate provision which he has made for every possible need that arises from his purposes or the contingencies of man's life.

God's continuing creativity is seen in the redemptive program in which he first re-creates man. Then God reclaims the barren desert, building the habitations of men as the City and Kingdom of God through the help of dedicated men and women. Christian stewardship becomes meaningful for Christians through the lordship of Jesus Christ. It is through him that we have a complete and full revelation of the nature and purpose of God. Through him we have access to, and fellowship with, such a purposeful God; and through our acceptance of God's sovereignty in the lordship of Jesus Christ we are initiated into God's great redemptive purpose that we may work with him.

This lordship of Christ is important for man because it gives life its true meaning, and defines the material universe in its proper relationship to man and God. The universe is important only as it helps us to serve God. Man can achieve his real manhood and stature only as he becomes an honest, responsible, and faithful manager of God's things for God's end under the lordship of Jesus Christ. He finds his true freedom through the design and control of God's will in Christ.

Witnessing

Then there is that sacred obligation to be a witness for Jesus Christ. Let us think of it for a moment. How was it you came to know about Jesus? How did it come to pass that you decided finally to give yourself to Jesus and to join the church? Was it because someone came to your home and talked with you personally about it? Maybe that person was a Sunday school teacher, a friend, a businessman, or a housewife who loved Jesus and wanted to share him with you. Perhaps you would not have made your decision if that friend of Christ had not called on you. That person may not have been a professional Christian worker. He may not have been trained in theology. He probably came to see you with the same timidity that you would feel if you were to do the same thing for someone else. But the point is, you learned of Jesus because someone else cared enough to witness for him. Remember: Christ is depending on you to do his work today.

In the early days of Christianity, the first impulse of those whom Jesus called was to go and tell others about him. Andrew found his brother, Simon Peter, and said to him, "We have found the Messiah," and he brought him to Jesus (John 1: 40-42). Philip found Nathaniel and said, "We have found him of whom Moses in the law and also the prophets wrote, Jesus of Nazareth" (John 1:45). Ever since that time the gospel has been handed down from one generation to another by Christians who cared enough to witness.

Honoré Willsie Morrow wrote an inspiring story of the life of Adoniram Judson. The study of his intrepid, selfless labors so inspired her that it brought her to Jesus. "Adoniram Judson is the best friend I ever had," she said. "He took my hand and put it into the hand of Jesus Christ." So can your life and your testimony lead someone to Jesus Christ.

Many churches today employ a plan called Home Visitation Evangelism. This method has resulted in thousands being won to Jesus Christ and active church membership. It is a way whereby members of the church are trained to do personal work in a friendly, effective way right in the homes of their prospects. This plan has proved a blessing to many of the people who have engaged in it, as well as to those whom they have visited. When this plan was introduced in our church several years ago, one of the men said: "This is real fun. Why hasn't someone told me about this before? The only kind of visiting I ever was asked to do before was in a financial canvass." These people, ordinary people just like you, went out from our church and secured definite commitments for Christ. As a result of their efforts over five hundred people were led to Christ in four years' time.

"You shall be my witnesses," said Jesus, "in Jerusalem [that is, at home] and in all Judea and Samaria [the surrounding areas] and to the end of the earth" (Acts 1:8). Thus Jesus, at the same time that he commissioned his disciples, set forth your responsibility and mine to spread the gospel everywhere.

Praying

You have also a responsibility to pray. Here at the beginning of your Christian life and your church affiliation, start the practice of daily prayer. Your prayers may be joined with those offered by other members of your family at the morning breakfast table or in the evening. Or they may be made by you privately upon arising, to meet the day at your best. They may be made before retiring, so that your rest may be more beneficial. Choose whatever time is best for you. But make your prayer life regular, if you would have it be most helpful.

You need not hesitate because of a fear that you do not know how to pray. The worth of a prayer is not determined by its grammatical correctness or by the beauty of its wording. Too many prayers unconsciously are made to a human audience. The worth of a prayer is determined by its sincerity. "Prayer is the soul's sincere desire." The main thing is to speak with God about the things that trouble you. Do not be deceived into thinking that there is no value in putting your needs into words. Although one's thoughts should be prayerful at all times, such thinking cannot be made a substitute for definite prayer. There is real value in expressing your deepest needs and thoughts. Furthermore, prayer must be intelligible and not meaningless repetition. I fear we are in danger of this error more than we realize.

A young husband, having been reared in a Christian home, determined at the outset of his married life that he would have prayer in his home. He had been deeply impressed by his father's example in this regard. However, his level of petition rarely exceeded the usual trite expressions. For instance, he prayed, "O Lord, be with the sick and afflicted." One morning, shortly after this prayer custom had been inaugurated, his wife naïvely asked him, "John, who are the sick and afflicted you have been praying for?" "Why, dear," he stammered, "I don't know; that is, I don't know of anyone in particular." "Oh," she responded in disappointment, "I purchased some jars of preserves yesterday and I thought I would call on some of the people you have been praying for and leave them something."

I fear also that far too much of our praying is on the begging level. If we fail by every other means to get something we want very much, we think we can fall back on prayer as a last resort. Then, if we fail to receive the thing we prayed for, we feel that God is not good. We try to use God as a means to an end, and we blame God if we fail.

In his teaching regarding prayer (Luke 11), Jesus counseled his disciples to ask for the coming of the Kingdom and for obedience to the will of God. He bade them to seek the forgiving heart and to cultivate the habit of avoiding temptation. Then he told them a story of a man who was disturbed by a visitor at midnight. Unable to set food before his unexpected guest, he went to a neighbor's house and beat upon the door loudly. In spite of the neighbor's irritation and unwillingness to give assistance, this man kept on knocking until he achieved his desire. Then Jesus said, "Ask, and it will be given you; seek, and you will find; knock, and it will be opened to you. . . . What father among you, if his son asks for a fish, will instead of a fish give him a serpent; or if he asks for an egg, will give him a scorpion? If you then, who are evil, know how to give good gifts to your children, how much more will the Heavenly Father give the Holy Spirit to those who ask him?" (Luke 11:9-13).

Upon first consideration this passage seems to encourage asking for *things*. It speaks of food. However, at the very end of this great lesson, our Lord speaks of the gift of the Holy Spirit in answer to prayer. People think they need many things, when in the last analysis they do not need things; they need God. They need the presence of God in their lives; they need the assurance which the presence of God gives. That is what is meant by the Holy Spirit being given in answer to prayer.

James declared: "You do not have, because you do not ask. You ask and do not receive, because you ask wrongly, to spend it on your passions" (James 4:2-3).

The highest and deepest benefit that one can receive from prayer is strength and courage to live triumphantly each day. A point at which we frequently err is indicated by James when he says that we ask in order that we may consume what we receive on our lusts. Dr. George A. Buttrick, in his helpful book entitled *Prayer*, points out that when a man prays he exposes himself to the promptings of God, and by so doing becomes less susceptible to the low persuasions of the world. True prayer, he explains, both illumines and purifies faith. It is an expression of confidence in God.

When we pray, there is a time to speak and there is a time to be still. One must be still if he is to know the will of God for himself with any certainty. He must be quiet to hear the "still, small voice." Prayer is communion in its deepest sense. It is the communion of your spirit with God's Spirit. After one has poured out one's heart to God, it is marvelous how in quiet meditation thinking becomes straightened, decisions become apparent, and vision becomes clarified. One can begin to think clearly and honestly when his mind has been elevated and his heart has been emptied of its burden through confession of the lips. Those who do not pray, do not experience this clarifying of thought, this purifying of motives, and this understanding and disciplining of self that come to those who pray in spirit and in truth.

We have a Christian responsibility to pray for others. "Pray one for another," James told his brethren, "that you may be healed" (James 5:16). Praying for others will enlarge the boundaries of your own soul. It will cleanse your thoughts of the evil spirit of envy and spite, for how can we think ill of one for whom we pray? It will bless the one for whom you pray more than you can realize.

Worshiping

You have a responsibility to worship. Worship keeps the soul of your church alive. Worship keeps the fires of inspiration burning.

Your church is set in your community to shine as a lighthouse for Jesus Christ. It will be such a lighthouse only so long as its members continue faithful in the matter of public worship. When the people of God begin to forsake the house of God on the Lord's Day, then God's work begins to languish and the light begins to fail. Faithful attendance upon the worship services of your church is necessary to the carrying out of your responsibility.

For that reason, view with suspicion every excuse, however reasonable it may seem, that occurs to you for evading the responsibility of worship. Some plausible reason may suggest itself to you for missing church "just this Sunday." It may be an unusual number of home responsibilities. It may be heavy school assignments. It may be visitors. But whatever it is, ask yourself the question: "Does this *have* to keep me from church? Isn't there some other time this can be done?"

In reading an account of the life and character of George Washington, I found that worship had a regular place upon his calendar. Mount Vernon was the center of a brilliant social life, and Washington had his social obligations along with everyone else, but no visitors or overnight guests ever kept him from church. He invited his guests to go to church *with* him; he did not permit their presence to keep him from attending. He worshiped with regularity, even though it meant traveling several miles by coach or on horseback.

The first hint of any dissatisfaction with the Christian life or with the church you have joined appears when you begin to miss its worship services. So long as you attend with regularity, you will continue to grow as a Christian. But when you cease attending, you will soon begin to find fault with the church, the minister, and the people. This does not mean necessarily that you have any real reason to find fault with them. It means rather that you are finding fault with yourself and are trying to ease your conscience by transferring the blame to someone else. You have a responsibility to keep up regular worship.

Continuing

You have a responsibility to continue in your loyalty to your church and to your Lord.

You may not always live in the community where you now reside. In fact, it may be that you will move a number of times during your life. What are you going to do about your church membership when you move from place to place?

Right here, let me explain that during recent years our churches have lost thousands of members due to the shifting of large masses of our population. Many church members who moved their belongings from one community to another failed to move their church membership to a church in the community where they took up their new abode. As a result they have become lost to the churches, to themselves, and to their Lord.

In our Baptist churches we have a system whereby you may move your membership from one church to another whenever it becomes necessary for you to change your place of residence. Many new members do not know this. A young woman once asked me, "When I move to another city and want to join a church there, do I have to be baptized again?" The answer is, No. When you move to another community, it is best for you to look up the Baptist church nearest your new home, and attend it the very first Sunday you are there. Do not put it off because you are busy, or because you do not know anyone. One of the best ways to become acquainted in a new community is to go to church. Do not wait for the pastor or some of the members to find out by chance that you are there. That is not fair either to them or to yourself. Take the initiative. Go to this church and tell the pastor that you wish to join. He will then write your former pastor and make a request for what is called a church letter. A church letter is a statement from your former church that you have been a member in good and regular standing, and are at your own request dismissed by it to unite with the church in the community where you now reside. If there is no Baptist church in your new community, then unite with some other church where you can sincerely worship and carry out the spirit of your convictions and beliefs.

Note that a church letter is a statement from one *church* to another *church*. It is not good Baptist polity to grant a letter without designating on it the church the individual is joining. Church letters should not be granted to an individual to carry in his "trunk," or keep in a drawer or desk, or perhaps in his Bible. A church letter vouches for active membership and anticipates active membership in the new situation. Otherwise, it is valueless and lacks integrity.

Do not put off transferring your membership because you have become so much attached to the church in what was your home town, or because you are so fond of its pastor, or have so many friends there. That is a mistaken loyalty. You cannot effectively serve your former church when you no longer live where you can attend it. Give your loyalty, devotion, service, and support to the church in the place where you are now living. Become a part of its life. Unite with it and serve God in it. You will quickly come to feel at home in it. If our churches are to continue to witness as they should for Christ, you should see to it that your church membership does not lapse or become inactive.

Above all, do not become discouraged. Discouragement is the young Christian's worst enemy.

It is said that the Devil once decided to go out of business. He displayed all of his tools and put price tags upon them. Prospective buyers began to examine the articles. One queer, wedge-shaped instrument aroused their curiosity. It was priced far above all the others. "Why is this so much higher?" they asked. "It isn't attractive at all." "That," replied the Devil, "is my most valuable tool. It is called Discouragement. I can get results with it when everything else fails. With it I can pry my way into a man's heart and make him feel that it is useless for him to try any longer."

Now, I have been discussing your responsibilities. I have spoken of your serving in your church, of your learning and growing in the Christian life, of your giving of your means to the carrying on of Jesus' work, of your witnessing to others of that which has come to you from others, and of your praying and worshiping and continuing. All these are necessary, if Jesus' prayer for world redemption is to have fulfillment. These are sacred responsibilities. But they are more. They are also a source of blessing in your own life. All that you expend in the ways which I have mentioned—serving, learning, giving, witnessing, praying, worshiping, and continuing—will come back to you a hundredfold in personal enrichment. While you are helping others you will be helping yourself also. An active Christian is a happy Christian.

For your information and reference I am adding to this

chapter a copy of the covenant which has been adopted by most Baptist churches and which sets forth those things which the members have agreed together to do.

CHURCH COVENANT

Having been led, as we believe, by the Spirit of God to receive the Lord Jesus Christ as our Savior, and on the profession of our faith, having been baptized in the name of the Father, and of the Son, and of the Holy Ghost, we do now in the presence of God, angels, and this assembly, most solemnly and joyfully enter into covenant with one another, as one body in Christ.

We engage, therefore, by the aid of the Holy Spirit, to walk together in Christian love; to strive for the advancement of this church in knowledge, holiness, and comfort; to promote its prosperity and spirituality; to sustain its worship, ordinances, discipline, and doctrines; to contribute cheerfully and regularly to the support of the ministry, the expenses of the church, the relief of the poor, and the spread of the gospel through all nations.

We also engage to maintain family and secret devotion; to educate our children religiously; to seek the salvation of our kindred and acquaintances; to walk circumspectly in the world; to be just in our dealings, faithful in our engagements, and exemplary in our deportment; to avoid all tattling, backbiting, and excessive anger; to abstain from the sale and use of intoxicating drink as a beverage, and to be zealous in our efforts to advance the kingdom of our Savior.

We further engage to watch over one another in brotherly love; to remember each other in prayer; to aid each other in sickness and distress; to cultivate Christian sympathy in feeling and courtesy in speech; to be slow to take offense, but always ready for reconciliation, and mindful of the rules of our Savior to secure it without delay.

We moreover engage that, when we remove from this place, we will as soon as possible unite with some other church where we can carry out the spirit of this covenant and the principles of God's Word.

QUESTIONS FOR DISCUSSION

1. In what sense is Jesus dependent upon us? Did your commitment to Jesus as Master include a willingness to serve in your church? If not, why not? If so, why?

2. What is the meaning to you of the Parable of the Talents? What are the possibilities for Christian training in your church? How are you using them?

3. What do you believe is the scriptural method of giving?

4. Do you wish to win others to Christ? Have you made any efforts to do so?

5. What are your prayer habits? What are your Bible study habits? How can they be improved?

6. What part does prayer play in living a successful Christian life? What part does church worship play in it?

PROJECTS AND REPORTS

1. Report on the leadership education program of your church.

2. Report on your church's method of every-member financial enlistment.

3. Report on your church's efforts in Youth and Discipleship Evangelism.

4. Report on your church's efforts in Home Visitation Evangelism.

5. Report on your church's method of transferring memberships.

6. Study and discuss the church covenant.

CHAPTER IV

Our Beliefs and Practices

The Principal Baptist Beliefs

If it is a Baptist church which you are planning to join, you have a right to know, and I am sure you will want to know, what Baptists believe. Baptists have many views in common with other evangelical Christians; for example, they believe in the existence of God, in the divinity of Christ, in Christ's death for man's sins, and in Christ's resurrection from the dead. These tenets are familiar and need not be discussed here. This chapter, therefore, will be devoted to those beliefs which are distinctive of Baptists and which constitute the reason for the existence of Baptists as a separate denomination. Six such beliefs may be mentioned.

1. Baptists hold that the Holy Scriptures, being the Word of God, constitute the supreme authority in all matters of religion. No man, be he pope or preacher, has the right to put his word ahead of that of the Scriptures. The Scriptures speak for God. They have the final word. Furthermore, no church has the right to presume to take the place of God's Word in spiritual matters; no church is at liberty to propose rules and regulations that are in conflict with the spirit and teaching of the New Testament. The Bible itself, rather than any creed or human interpretation of the Bible, is the final authority in all matters pertaining to the soul. The other distinctive principles really grow out of this first one.

2. A second distinctive principle is that of the separation of church and state. The Baptist position in this matter is based upon the spirit of New Testament Christianity. Peter, when faced with the threat of the Jewish Council, declared, "We must obey God rather than men" (Acts 5:29). Jesus advised, "Render therefore to Caesar the things that are Caesar's, and to God the things that are God's" (Matt. 22:21).

This position is based also on sound logic. Wherever there has been a union of the church and the civil government, corruption and evil have come out of it. In church history, the periods of greatest religious decline have been those when the alliance between the church and the state has been the strongest. The atheistic philosophy of communism might not have arisen in Russia to plague the world if there had not been in that unfortunate country an unwholesome union of church and state. From the very beginning of their history, Baptists have protested whenever the state has attempted to control the consciences of men; and, conversely, Baptists have insisted that no religious group has the right to receive special favors at the hand of the state.

3. A third principle is the independence of each local church. Baptists reject the Roman Catholic idea (and the related ideas of certain Protestant groups) that there should be a strongly centralized form of church government under one head, and with all the member churches of this organization doing whatever this central government demands. The Roman Catholic view is contrary to New Testament belief and practice. "Neither be called masters," warned Jesus, "for you have one master, the Christ. He who is greatest among you shall be your servant" (Matt. 22:10-11).

Each Baptist church retains its full autonomy. Its only Master is Christ. This independence may seem to make for weakness. An attorney once remarked to me: "I think if and when I join a church I shall join the Roman Catholic Church. It has the power of organization behind it." "Did you ever stop to think," I reminded him, "that when the little first-century church turned the world upside down and conquered pagan Rome, it had no powerful organization behind it? Its power was an inner power, the inner power of conviction that it had the answer to the world's need; namely, that Jesus was the hope of the world, and that he still lived." "I hadn't thought of that," the lawyer confessed.

Baptists believe that a church should have the right to choose its own pastor and to manage its own affairs. They have no bishops, no high church officials, and no hierarchical form of church government. They have state and national organizations, but these bodies are agencies of the individual churches, created by them and obedient to them.

Although the Baptist churches retain their independence, they are held together by brotherly love, and by their devotion to a common task, the Great Commission which their risen Lord has given them. In the accomplishing of their tasks, they see the value of working together, and they count it a privilege to co-operate with other Baptist churches, and also with churches of other denominations that have the same Christian objectives. The Boards and Conventions which the Baptist churches have set up are means by which they give their gifts and efforts greater effectiveness.

4. Baptists believe in the priesthood of the believer. That is, they hold that every believer has direct access to God, and therefore is not dependent on the intervention or intercession of a priest or any other human agent. They object to the idea, held by many, that man, being sinful, cannot approach God, but must secure the services of a priest to intercede with God on his behalf. Baptists contend that every believer is privileged to be his own priest, and that he should not expect any other Christian to perform his religious duties for him. Furthermore, the New Testament makes no mention of any prayers being offered to Mary or to any saint, such as now are offered in the Roman Catholic Church.

5. A fifth distinctive tenet is that of religious freedom. This has been implied in all that has been stated above. Baptists believe that everyone should have the right to worship God in accordance with his own understanding and convictions as to what God desires. This belief is so much a commonplace in America today that the statement of it sounds trite. But this has not always been the case, and there are still lands in which Christians are persecuted, if they undertake to exercise this right. Religious freedom is something that political tyrants have always sought to keep from the people. The religious freedom we enjoy in America has been bought at a great price. It is a precious heritage. Baptists have been leaders in the struggle for religious freedom, and will continue to contend for it.

Bancroft, the eminent historian, has stated that freedom of conscience, unlimited freedom of mind, was from the first the trophy of the Baptists. A modern writer maintains that Roger Williams, founder of the first Baptist church in America, contributed to the making of the United States hardly less than a dozen Presidents. In colonial days the Massachusetts courts had jurisdiction over religious as well as civil affairs. One had to be a member of the established church to vote on civil matters. But Roger Williams, when banished from Massachusetts for his independent views, established a religious democracy at Providence which was governed by the people, and which granted full political and religious freedom to all.

The Baptists were instrumental in securing the adoption of the First Amendment to the Constitution of the United States. Its opening words are: "Congress shall make no law respecting an establishment of religion, or prohibiting the free exercise thereof." Cathcart, an early church historian, shows that the Baptists were the only denominational group that pressed for the adoption of this amendment. The Quakers did not ask for it. John Adams and the Congregationalists did not want it. The Episcopalians did not desire it. It was going too far for the Presbyterians of Revolutionary times. The Baptists asked for it through Washington.

6. A sixth distinctive belief is the baptism of believers only. Contrary to much popular thinking, this distinctive conviction is not immersion, as over against sprinkling; it is immersion of *believers only*. And this brings us to a discussion of the ordinances. When we have considered the ordinances, we shall be better able to understand the Baptist position regarding believer's baptism.

The Two Ordinances

What is an ordinance? An ordinance is a ceremony which the Lord has prescribed and bidden the church to observe. Baptists believe that there are only two ordinances; baptism and the Lord's Supper. Baptists further believe that these ordinances, although of sacred origin and significance and very meaningful to the sincere Christian, do not of themselves impart divine grace or Christian character to those who receive them. Baptists do not consider these ordinances to be sacraments. A "sacrament," in the view of certain Christian bodies, because of its divine character imparts some special merit to the recipient. The Roman Catholic Church lists seven sacraments: baptism, the eucharist (Mass), confirmation, penance, extreme unction, ordination, and marriage. Baptists hold that this belief in sacraments is both contrary to the teachings of the New Testament and savors of a superstitious dependence on magic.

1. *The Ordinance of Baptism.* Why baptize? Who told us we should? Is there anything authoritative in connection with baptism? These are valid questions. Yet too often they are passed over because we feel that they are so simple that everyone must know the answer.

When Jesus had grown to manhood, he heard about the ministry of John the Baptist, who was calling upon men to repent and be baptized. Jesus knew then that the hour had struck when he should come out of his obscurity and begin his world-shaking, three-year ministry. So, although our Lord had nothing of which to repent, he came to the river Jordan where John was baptizing and asked to be baptized. John looked at him in astonishment and remonstrated, "I need to be baptized by you, and do you come to me?" "Let it be so now," Jesus insisted; "for thus it is fitting for us to fulfill all righteousness" (Matt. 3:14-15). Jesus set the precedent for baptism by being baptized himself.

In addition to this, Jesus left it as one of his last commandments to his followers. Matthew states that the eleven disciples went to Galilee to the mountain Jesus had indicated, and when they saw him there they began to worship him. I believe that Jesus and those eleven disciples constituted the very beginning of the Christian church. Jesus said, "All authority in heaven and on earth has been given to me. Go therefore and make disciples of all nations, baptizing them in the name of the Father and of the Son and of the Holy Spirit, teaching them to observe all that I have commanded you" (Matt. 28: 18-20). We baptize today because Jesus was baptized, and because he said that all who believe on him should be baptized.

Immediately following Jesus' baptism, it became the practice of Jesus' disciples to baptize all who became his avowed followers. John, the writer of the Fourth Gospel, affirms that Jesus and his disciples went into the land of Judea. There "he remained with them and baptized" (John 3:22). John further states that "when the Lord knew that the Pharisees had heard that Jesus was making and baptizing more disciples than John (although Jesus himself did not baptize, but only his disciples), he left Judea" (John 4:1-2). The point to observe here is that it was the custom even then to baptize those who had become disciples.

Baptism was the established practice of the first-century Christian church. On the day of Pentecost, Peter, filled with the Holy Spirit, fervently addressed a great throng of the Jewish people. He climaxed his sermon with the stirring words, "God has made him both Lord and Christ, this Jesus whom you crucified." And Luke, the writer of Acts, states that "when they heard this they were cut to the heart, and said to Peter and the rest of the apostles, 'Brethren, what shall we do?' And Peter said to them, 'Repent and be baptized every one of you in the name of Jesus Christ.'" Luke then relates that "those who received his word were baptized, and there were added that day about three thousand souls" (Acts 2:36-41).

The apostles instructed their converts to be baptized. This is the clear teaching of the New Testament. Luke points out (Acts 8:12-13) that when the Samaritans believed the good news which Philip the evangelist preached about Jesus Christ, they were baptized, both men and women. Even Simon, the magician, believed and was baptized.

One of the most interesting accounts of conversion and baptism is that of the Ethiopian eunuch who was on his way back to the court of his queen. When Philip saw him, he heard the voice of the Spirit of God say, "Go up and join this chariot." Philip obeyed. He found the man reading the prophecy of Isaiah at the fifty-third chapter. "About whom, pray, does the prophet say this?" queried the Ethiopian. Luke says that Philip then taught him about Jesus. "And as they went along the road they came to some water, and the eunuch asked, 'See, here is water! What is to prevent my being baptized?' And he commanded the chariot to stop, and they both went down into the water, Philip and the eunuch, and he baptized him" (Acts 8:36-38). It is most significant that this man, although an Ethiopian, knew that it was the custom of the church to baptize those who believed on Christ. This is substantial evidence that baptism was the well-known practice of the Christians even in that early day.

Saul, who became Paul, was baptized very shortly after his dramatic conversion experience (Acts 9:18-19).

When Peter had been persuaded that the gospel was for the Gentiles as well as for the Jews, he went to Caesarea to the home of Cornelius and proclaimed the good news of the risen Christ. It is said that the Holy Spirit fell on all who heard his words. Then Peter declared, "Can any one forbid water for baptizing these people who have received the Holy Spirit just as we have?" (Acts 10:47). Then he commanded them to be baptized in the name of Jesus Christ.

Paul and Silas and their company, as missionaries, carried the gospel far into Asia Minor, then crossed the straits and came to Philippi, the leading city of Macedonia and a Roman colony. On the Sabbath they went outside the gate of the city and sought out a spot by the riverside used by the Jews as a place of prayer. They sat down and talked with the women who came there. One of them was Lydia. The Lord opened her heart to the words of Paul, and she and her whole household were baptized (Acts 16:11-15).

Having incurred the wrath of some of the citizens of Philippi, Paul and Silas were thrown into prison. An earthquake freed them and brought the trembling jailer to them on his knees, crying, "What must I do to be saved?" And Paul answered, " 'Believe in the Lord Jesus, and you will be saved, you and your household.' And they spoke the word of the Lord to him and to all that were in his house. . . . And he was baptized at once, with all his family" (Acts 16:30-33).

Luke also tells of the baptism of Crispus and of many other Corinthians who believed (Acts 18:8).

Now we may ask, who should be baptized? A person should not be baptized unless he has believed on Jesus Christ, has given himself of his own free will to Christ, is trusting Christ for full and complete salvation, and is ready to serve Christ. According to New Testament example and teaching, only a person who has truly believed on Christ may rightly be baptized.

Infants are not proper subjects for baptism, and for a number of reasons. For one reason, there is no New Testament instance of the baptism of infants. In every instance, the baptism is of a person who has received the word of the Lord. Surely this can mean only one who is old enough to hear and understand gospel truth. Family groups are mentioned, but infants are not. In addition, infants are not ready for baptism, for baptism presupposes that the individual knows the difference between right and wrong, and is, therefore, capable of voluntarily confessing his sinfulness and receiving the forgiveness of God through his faith in Jesus Christ. Infants, while inheriting the nature of lost humanity to sin, are themselves still innocent of overt sin. Jesus affirmed, "Unless you turn and become like children, you will never enter the kingdom of heaven" (Matt. 18:3). The baptism of infants, accordingly, rests upon two incorrect assumptions: that the infant is sinful, and that baptism will save his soul. Both teachings are contrary to New Testament thought. Baptism, no matter by whom performed, will not save the soul. Only the renewing of the Spirit of God will do that. "He saved us, not because of deeds done by us in righteousness," wrote Paul, "but in virtue of his own mercy, by the washing of regeneration and renewal in the Holy Spirit" (Titus 3:5).

We read of mothers who brought their children to Jesus, but they brought them, not to be baptized, but to be blessed. The dedication of babies is a beautiful thing so long as it has a meaning to the parents, but dedication is wholly different from baptism. The practice of infant baptism arose early in the history of the church when the erroneous idea came into prominence that baptism was essential to salvation. When it proved inconvenient or impossible always to baptize by immersion, the substitution of affusion or sprinkling was adopted and persists to this day, but it is not New Testament baptism.

The Baptist emphasis, however, is not primarily upon the mode (although they hold that immersion is the only New Testament form); the Baptist emphasis is upon the baptism of believers only. They stand for *believer's* baptism, and say that only those who are believers on Jesus Christ should receive it. This is made clear in every one of the instances that have been cited above. Those who were baptized on the day of Pentecost were repentant believers. Those whom Jesus and his disciples baptized were disciples first. In his commission our Lord commands that his followers first make disciples and then baptize them. Simon was a believer before he was baptized, and the Ethiopian had received the teaching about Jesus as the sin-bearer of the world. Saul was first converted and then baptized. Cornelius and his household, as well as his guests, had been filled with the Spirit of God before they were baptized. Lydia, on hearing the words of Paul, had opened her heart to Jesus Christ. The Philippian jailer, along with his household, had been shown the way of salvation; and Crispus and other Corinthians had believed on the Christ. It is believer's baptism only.

But how should one be baptized? Baptists hold that New Testament baptism is immersion in water. Many reasons can be advanced in support of this view. We shall examine a few of them.

Our English word "baptize" comes from a Greek word *baptizo,* which means to immerse, to dip, or to plunge. In the New Testament, the word has no other meaning. In our English versions of the New Testament, this Greek word has not really been translated; it has merely been brought over (transliterated) into English and made a part of our English speech.

That the verb *baptizo* means to immerse is acknowledged by practically all New Testament scholars, even though they are connected with churches which do not now practice immersion. Here are a few of many such statements:

Martin Luther, the Protestant reformer, said: "In the primitive church, baptism was a total immersion, or burial, as it were."

John Calvin, Presbyterian theologian, said: "Baptize signifies to immerse, and it is certain that immersion was the practice of the ancient church."

Thomas Cranmer, Archbishop of Canterbury, said: "By baptism we die with Christ, and are buried, as it were."

John Wesley, founder of Methodism, said: "Buried with him, alluding to baptizing by immersion, according to the custom of the first church."

Doctor Chalmers, first moderator of the Free Church, Scotland, said: "Baptism is immersion."

Doctor Pain, Congregational professor of ecclesiastical history, said: "Immersion was the baptism of the Christian church for thirteen centuries."

Dean Stanley, Episcopalian, said: "In the apostolic age those who came to baptism came in full age, and of their own choice. Those who were baptized were immersed in the water."

Dr. Adam Clark, a Methodist Bible commentator, said: "The mode of administering baptism was by immersion, the whole body being put under water."

Philip Schaff, a Presbyterian church historian, said: "Immersion was unquestionably the original form of baptism."

Bishop White, Anglican, said: "Immersion was the primitive and apostolic baptism. Immersion was the only mode of baptism in the early church. God in his providence has permitted the Baptist denomination to restore the long-lost primitive mode of immersion, teaching the death, burial and resurrection of Christ."

These eminent scholars could not well write otherwise in the light of the historical records which have come down to us from the earliest Christian centuries. For example, the *Didache,* or *Teaching of the Twelve,* was written quite early in the second century. It describes baptism as immersion, and permits affusion (pouring) only when necessary, as in the case of sickness. Other church fathers of the second century are equally clear in their statements. In fact, the Roman Catholic Church did not entirely abandon immersion until about the thirteenth or fourteenth century on the Continent, and not until the early sixteenth century in England. However, the Roman Catholic Church had begun the practice of infant baptism as early as the third century, possibly as early as the late second century. It is significant that the Eastern Orthodox Catholic churches, although they baptize infants, still practice immersion.

Immersion, and no other form, preserves the full meaning of the ordinance of baptism. The believer, on being baptized, shows symbolically that he has died to sin. Hence, Paul writes, "We were buried therefore with him by baptism into death" (Rom. 6:4). In the Douay Version of the Bible (the English version which is approved by the Roman Catholic Church) there is an interesting note on this verse. The annotation states that the verse refers "to the primitive mode of baptism by immersion."

Circumstances attending the rite similarly indicate immersion. Matthew says that Jesus came up out of the water after he was baptized. Luke says that both Philip and the eunuch went into the water and then Philip baptized him. John says that John the Baptist was baptizing at Aenon near Salim, "because there was much water there."

And now, what does baptism signify? First of all, it may be well to emphasize the fact that baptism is the door to membership in the church. During the days of the New Testament church, believers were considered members of the church (which they called "the body of Christ" or "the called-out ones") when they had been baptized. They were not considered members of the church prior to their baptism. Luke states in Acts that they who received the word of Peter were baptized, and "there were added that day about three thousand souls" (Acts 2:41); he tells us also that "the Lord added to their number day by day those who were being saved" (Acts 2:47). Paul affirms that all the members of the church are one body, that the body is Christ's, and that by one Spirit they were all baptized into that one body (1 Cor. 12:12-13, 27).

Baptism, however, has another profound meaning. It pictures symbolically the death, burial, and resurrection of Jesus Christ. Paul says, "We were buried therefore with him by baptism into death, so that as Christ was raised from the dead by the glory of the Father, we too might walk in newness of life" (Rom. 6:4). Every baptismal service, therefore, is a picture of the death of Christ for us, and of his glorious resurrection from the dead.

Beautiful though this symbolism is, baptism has a still deeper significance. It also symbolizes the fact that the believer, through Christ, is dead to the old life of sin and alive to the new life of righteousness. This is the second meaning of the verse quoted just above. Baptism is a symbol of the inner purification wrought by the indwelling Spirit of God. The thought of resurrection here goes beyond that of the present spiritual resurrection of the soul when one becomes a believer in Jesus; it points to the great resurrection beyond the grave and affirms that if one has experienced the spiritual resurrection today, he will with Jesus experience the great resurrection of tomorrow. Paul continues, "For if we have been united with him in a death like his, we shall certainly be united with him in a resurrection like his" (Rom. 6:5).

Some time ago there appeared in *Baptist Leader* an article by Grace Vernon in which she told of some of her vivid experiences on the mission field in India. Their first convert was a caste Hindu. He had been arrogant and proud, regarding Christians as dirt under his feet. However, he was finally won to the Christian faith. But on the day of his baptism his family conducted a funeral for him. They burned his body in effigy and confiscated all his property. "I'm sorry," said the missionary sympathetically, "that the joy of this day of your baptism must be mixed with grief because of your family." "It is not," he quickly responded. "Don't you see that by holding a funeral for me they only remind me that on this day my old self is dying!"

2. *The Ordinance of the Lord's Supper.* The Lord's Supper, often called communion, is the second ordinance recognized by Baptists. Whereas the believer is baptized but once, he partakes of the Lord's Supper, if possible, whenever that ordinance is observed by the church. Most Baptist churches observe communion once a month, others every three months, and a few even less frequently. There is no definite scriptural precedent as to the frequency of observance.

As Christian baptism was prefigured in the Jewish baptism of repentance and purification, so the Lord's Supper was prefigured in the Jewish Feast of the Passover. In the Passover observance unleavened bread and unfermented grape juice (the "fruit of the vine") were employed. These same "elements" are used in the Lord's Supper, but in the Lord's Supper they take on a new and larger significance.

It was on the Thursday night of his last week, the night on which later he was betrayed into the hands of his enemies, that our Lord met with his disciples in the upper room of the home of a friend in Jerusalem. They met, at Jesus' bidding, to observe the Passover Feast after the manner of the Jews. At the conclusion of the feast, while they were still at the table, Jesus took a piece of the bread and said, "Take, eat; this is my body." Also, "he took a cup, and when he had given thanks he gave it to them, saying, 'Drink of it, all of you; for this is my blood of the covenant, which is poured out for many for the forgiveness of sins. I tell you I shall not drink again of this fruit of the vine until that day when I drink it new with you in my Father's kingdom'" (Matt. 26:26-29).

This is the origin of the Lord's Supper. We observe it in our churches because Jesus instituted it, and because he asked his disciples to observe it through all time. It is a memorial supper. Our observance of it is in remembrance of him. As the Passover feast reminded the Jewish people of their deliverance from bondage and death in Egypt, so the Lord's Supper reminds the Christian of his deliverance from sin and death by virtue of Christ's death and resurrection.

The apostle Paul, writing later, gives us this account of the institution of the Lord's Supper. "The Lord Jesus on the night when he was betrayed took bread, and when he had given thanks, he brake it, and said, 'This is my body which is broken for you. Do this in remembrance of me.' In the same way also the cup, after supper, saying, 'This cup is the new covenant in my blood. Do this, as often as you drink it, in remembrance of me.' For as often as you eat this bread and drink this cup you proclaim the Lord's death until he comes" (1 Cor. 11:23-26).

Now, the Lord's Supper further symbolizes the fact that Jesus is our source of life, both here and hereafter. Partaking of the Lord's Supper does not give that life. The Lord's Supper stands for the truth that Christ gives us that life. This is the force of Jesus' statement: "I am the living bread which came down from heaven; if any one eats of this bread, he will live for ever; and the bread which I shall give for the life of the world is my flesh. . . . He who eats my flesh and drinks my blood has eternal life, and I will raise him up at the last day" (John 6:51-54).

Jesus here is not saying that the actual partaking of his flesh and blood will give eternal life. Such an interpretation is absurd. Neither would he have us understand that partaking of the Lord's Supper will impart eternal life. He means that he himself was and is the source of life, and that one may partake of that life through faith and acceptance of him. The Lord's Supper is a portrayal of the fact that when you came to Jesus and accepted him, you partook of him and thus received eternal life. "I am the bread of life," Jesus said; "he who comes to me shall not hunger, and he who believes in me shall never thirst" (John 6:35). Thus, the Lord's Supper also reminds us that, as Christ is the giver of our spiritual life, so also he is the sustainer of it.

Furthermore, partaking of the Lord's Supper should remind us of our union with Christ. "He who eats my flesh and drinks my blood," Jesus affirmed, "abides in me and I in him" (John 6:56). Be sure to remember that partaking of the bread and the fruit of the vine does not impart this union. It is only the movement of your soul toward God through Christ and the opening of your heart to him that permits him to dwell within you.

Roman Catholics affirm that in the Mass the bread and the wine actually become the flesh and blood of Jesus. This is the view known as transubstantiation. They believe that Christ is truly present in the bread and wine, but that it is his spiritual presence, rather than any physical presence, of which the believer partakes. These teachings, Baptists believe, are in error. Jesus did say, "This is my body" and "This is my blood" when he referred to the bread and the cup, but he was still living in the flesh when he made those statements. Hence, the statements cannot be understood literally. He meant that we are to think of the bread and the cup as symbols of his flesh and blood, and nothing more.

The Lord's Supper is a church ordinance, and is to be observed by the assembled church. All the New Testament references indicate that it was observed only when the Christians were meeting together as a body of believers. Luke speaks of the followers of Jesus partaking of communion together (Acts 2:42). He indicates that the disciples came together on the first day of the week to break bread and hear Paul preach (Acts 20:7). Paul speaks of the fact that the Corinthian Christians, when they came together, were careless of their observance of the Lord's Supper. There are some Baptists who hold that, under special circumstances, the church may properly authorize its pastor to give communion to an individual; for example, to a shut-in or to a person in a hospital. Other Baptists hold that whatever help the communion might be to the recipient, this practice is liable to build up the belief that the Lord's Supper is a sacrament and that the bread and the cup, in themselves, are a means of grace.

The Lord's Supper is an ordinance for the church, not just for the clergy. The Roman Catholic Church withholds the cup from the congregation and limits it to the clergy only. However, that is contrary to New Testament teaching and practice. When Jesus gave the cup to his disciples, he told them all to drink of it.

Now, a word about the prerequisites for communion. Who may partake and who may not partake? Again we find the New Testament clear in its teachings. In the second chapter of Acts we find individuals who "devoted themselves to the apostles' teaching and fellowship, to the breaking of bread and prayers." Who were these people? They were those who had heard the preaching of Peter on the day of Pentecost and who had been convicted by it. They had cried, "What shall we do?" And Peter had replied, "Repent, and be baptized every one of you." They gladly received his word and were baptized, thus identifying themselves with the body of believers. After having done this, they were ready to receive communion. Communion is for believers only. There is no New Testament account of anyone receiving the bread and cup without first having professed his faith in the Lord Jesus Christ, having been baptized, and having thus identified himself with the Christians. In the early days of the post-apostolic age all nonbelievers were asked to leave the assembly of Christians before communion was taken. To take communion marked a person definitely as a baptized believer and as a possible object of official persecution.

The New Testament indicates further that one should not partake who does not have regard for the meaning of the ordinance. An abuse of the Lord's Supper had grown up among the Corinthian Christians. They were debasing it and rendering it meaningless. Some were actually eating and drinking to disgusting excess. "Whoever, therefore, eats the bread or drinks the cup of the Lord in an unworthy manner," Paul warned, "will be guilty of profaning the body and blood of the Lord. Let a man examine himself, and so eat of the bread and drink of the cup. For any one who eats and drinks without discerning the body eats and drinks judgment upon himself" (1 Cor. 11:27-29). In other words, even if you are a baptized believer in Christ, examine yourself before you partake to make certain that when you do, you will do so reverently and in memory of Jesus Christ.

"Therefore, my beloved," Paul entreated the Corinthians, "shun the worship of idols. . . . The cup of blessing which we bless, is it not a participation in the blood of Christ? The bread which we break, is it not a participation in the body of Christ? . . . You cannot drink the cup of the Lord and the cup of demons. You cannot partake of the table of the Lord and the table of demons. 'All things are lawful,' but not all things build up" (1 Cor. 10:14-23).

In other words, the bread and the cup represent our union with Jesus Christ. We cannot possibly be united with him when we serve evil, too. We cannot serve two masters. Since we cannot rightly partake of the Lord's Supper if our hearts have grown cold and critical, or if we have been living in sin, the recurring observance by the church of the Lord's Supper should remind us of our need to live consistent Christian lives and to keep ourselves in fellowship with our Lord.

I have told you all these things, not to prejudice you or to make you narrow-minded, but to inform you. Unfortunately there are thousands of Baptists who are poorly informed concerning their denomination and who are without any very definite beliefs and convictions.

QUESTIONS FOR DISCUSSION

1. Name some respects in which Baptist beliefs and practices differ from those of other denominations.

2. What is the significance of the ordinance of baptism?

3. What is the significance of the ordinance of the Lord's Supper?

4. Are these ideas concerning baptism and the Lord's Supper distinctive to the Baptists? Are they important enough to observe with fidelity?

5. What is meant by the term "the priesthood of believers"? What Roman Catholic doctrine does it contradict?

6. What is the distinction between a sacrament and an ordinance? Can baptism rightly be called a sacrament? Can the Lord's Supper rightly be called a sacrament?

7. Who may rightly participate in the observance of the Lord's Supper?

8. What is meant by the expression "baptismal regeneration"? Do Baptists believe in baptismal regeneration? Is the idea at variance with the doctrine of salvation by grace?

PROJECTS AND REPORTS

1. Find and discuss passages in the Book of Hebrews dealing with the priesthood of the believer.

2. Report on the position of your church respecting baptism and the Lord's Supper.

3. Report on baptism as understood and practiced by a church of another faith.

4. Report on the frequency with which your church observes the Lord's Supper.

CHAPTER V

My Church and My Denomination at Work

The Organization of My Church

By this time you have thought about the responsibilities of the Christian life. You have studied, in a general way, the nature and mission of the church; and you have been introduced to Baptist principles and beliefs. Let us now concentrate on the way the Baptist churches are organized to carry on the great work that Christ has left for us to do.

1. *The church you are joining has a pastor.* He holds the highest office in your church, but he is still one of the people. He is to be the preacher, the one who makes known by his sermons the gospel of Jesus Christ. He is to lead the congregation in its worship on the Lord's Day and at other appointed times. He is to be a personal counselor to the members of the church and is to help them with their individual problems, whether their problems are of a strictly religious nature or not. He is to be a wise and courageous Christian leader, one who is completely devoted to the work of Christ. He is to have general oversight of the church and of all its activities, but he is not to be in any sense a dictator. Instead, he is to be the "shepherd of the flock."

A young man chooses the ministry because he feels certain in his heart that God has called him for that work. He should then secure adequate training. Usually this means four years of college and three years in a theological seminary. Sometimes it is possible for him to serve in a pastoral capacity, either full or part-time, before completing his training. Such an arrangement will give him an opportunity to gain firsthand experience in church work and in dealing with people both within the church and outside of it. After this, if he shows evidence of possessing the necessary qualifications, the church of which he is a member will plan his ordination. It will invite the other churches of the association to which it belongs to send delegates who will constitute an ordination council.

The members of the council will then examine the candidate for the ministry. They will question him concerning his call, his Bible knowledge, and his doctrinal beliefs. If these representatives of the churches feel that he is of worthy character and is sufficiently prepared, they will recommend to the church that it proceed with his ordination. To be ordained means to be set apart officially for definite Christian work.

The pastor of the church you are joining was ordained in this way. He became pastor of your church because your church, by its vote, asked him to do so. He was not appointed by any denominational agency or official. When seeking a pastor, members of a Baptist church meet together, talk over possible persons, then vote to invite the one of their choice. The pastor is the choice of the members of the church, and he continues as pastor so long as his services are acceptable to them.

2. *Your church also has deacons.* It may have any number it chooses. A deacon, like the pastor, is chosen by vote of the church. Sometimes deacons are ordained and serve for life; more frequently they are elected for a term of years. The deacons administer the Lord's Supper. They also look after the spiritual welfare of the congregation, and help the pastor in visitation and in many other matters. Sometimes the deacons administer a church fund from which they give financial assistance to needy members. The deacons meet with the pastor to pray with him and to counsel with him concerning the things which will benefit the church.

3. *Your church also has trustees.* These men advise and protect the church in business matters. The laws of most states require that churches have such officials. They look after the church property, keep it in repair, and see that the necessary fuel and other supplies are on hand. Sometimes they have the responsibility of raising money for the support of the ministry and work of the church.

4. *Your church also has a clerk.* The clerk keeps a record of all actions taken at the business meetings of the church. He keeps an up-to-date list of the members of the church.

5. *Your church also has a treasurer.* He is the custodian of the funds of the church. He keeps an accurate record of all money received by the church, and pays it out, when authorized

to do so, to those causes which the church has approved.

These are the officers usually found in a Baptist church. Sometimes there are more. Sometimes a church will have a moderator. The moderator presides when business meetings are in session. Sometimes there is a financial secretary, who assists the treasurer by keeping a record of the weekly contributions of the members. There also may be a benevolence treasurer, who receives and pays out the money given for missionary causes. All these officers are chosen by a vote of the church.

6. *Your church also has a number of committees.* These committees, usually chosen by vote of the church, assist the pastor and help the church to carry on its work efficiently.

There is quite often a finance committee, which has the responsibility of raising the money needed by the church, thus relieving the trustees of that extra work. It approves all bills before the treasurer pays them, and otherwise looks after the financial interests of the church.

There may be a Christian education committee or a Board of Christian Education, which has charge of the general educational program of the church, including the Sunday church school, the vacation church school, training classes, youth work, etc.

Your church may have a missionary committee to promote missionary interest and giving for the cause of Christian missions at home and abroad.

There may be a committee on evangelism to see that a proper emphasis is placed upon winning people to Christ and the church by means of evangelistic meetings, personal interviews, and visitation in the homes.

Likewise, there may be a committee on stewardship, charged with the responsibility of teaching the principles of Christian stewardship and encouraging systematic giving.

There may be an advisory council, consisting of representatives from the board of deacons, the board of trustees, the board of Christian education, and the above-named committees as well as from the other organizations in the church. Such a large and representative committee can help to shape the overall policy of the church and aid in promoting the church's program.

Your church probably will have an annual business meeting at which the members will meet together to hear reports of work done during the year by the church and its organizations, to adopt a financial budget for the coming year, and to elect officers. In addition, there may be a business meeting every month or every quarter throughout the year. Special business meetings may be held whenever these are considered necessary.

7. *There are also other organizations within your church.* These organizations, which are a part of the church or are auxiliary to it, are designed to help the church carry on its work. The Sunday church school is a part of your church. There will be a Baptist Youth Fellowship, with young people meeting Sunday morning and evening and carrying out a week-day program. There may be organizations of boys and girls under twelve. There will likely be organizations for the men and women of the church to promote missionary and other types of work and for fellowship. Probably there will be a Men's Fellowship and a Woman's Mission Society. These organizations may elect their own officers and carry on their own work, yet they are a part of the total work of the church.

The History of My Denomination

Because the church which you are joining is a Baptist church, I believe you will be glad to read this very brief sketch of Baptist history. When you have done so, you will be better able to understand why the Baptist churches chose to set up the kind of denominational organization which they now have.

The churches of the first century were simple, informal organizations. At first, the Christians met for worship in private homes on the first day of the week, as well as at other times during the week. Christ was exalted as the head of the body, which was the church, and baptism and church membership followed repentance and faith in Christ.

But when the apostles had died, strange teachings began to creep in. In order to strengthen the churches and at the same time to protect the believers against persecution, the pastors in the largest cities were given greater authority over the congregations. In time, a system of bishops or leading churchmen grew up, which in the West resulted eventually in the recognition of the bishop of Rome as the supreme head of the church, or pope. This extreme centralization of authority which took place within the Roman Catholic Church proved unwholesome. It was harmful to the maintenance of true spirituality. At the same time, some pastors began to preach that baptism itself washes away sin; therefore infants were baptized lest they "die in their sins."

However, there were all along those who resisted these tendencies because they thought they were wrong. For example, there was during the second century a group of Christians who were known as Montanists. They said, "We reject infant baptism, the right to exercise power claimed by the bishop, and the idea of the episcopacy." Then later, a group of Christians, called Novatians, protested that the churches ought to be independent and that the pastors ought to be equal in dignity and authority. Yet another group of protestors was known as Donatists. "We believe in the independence of each church," they said. "We believe in the purity of church membership and reject infant baptism. We believe in the congregational form of church government, freedom of conscience, separation of church and state, and a regenerate church membership." All these groups practiced baptism by immersion. They were sorely persecuted, but they were loyal to their convictions and were not afraid to die for them, when need arose.

It is not possible to tell here the whole glorious story of the Waldensians, the Anabaptists, and other groups which in a still later day contended for many of the very views for which Baptists stand today. Certain of them sought to establish religious freedom. They believed in the Scriptures as the sole rule of faith and conduct, and in baptism by immersion, after repentance, as the door to church membership. They protested against the tyranny of the Roman Catholic Church and opposed that hierarchical form of church government. While it may not be possible to trace a direct historical connection between such early groups and the people who later became known everywhere as Baptists, those intrepid believers may be thought of as the spiritual ancestors of the present-day Baptists.

Hence, it is not strictly correct to say that the Baptists originated in, or at the time of, the Reformation of Martin Luther. Long before his day there had been men of Baptist persuasion. During the Reformation, and afterward, these early "Baptists," if we may call them such, were persecuted by both Roman Catholics and Protestants alike. Their origin and development cannot be explained as the work of any one man. They can be accounted for only in terms of loyalty to the Scriptures and of devotion to religious freedom and equality in Christ.

Baptists have had a long and honorable history. Today they have become a large and influential Christian body.

The Organization of My Denomination

Thus, you see, you are doing more than to join a particular church. You are identifying yourself with a great company of Baptists numbering in the millions. They are all over the world. In order to have fellowship with one another and to help one another, Baptists have set up state and national organizations.

The Baptists of Great Britain are organized in a Baptist Union. So also are the Baptists of Canada. In the United States there are a number of Baptist groups, called Conventions. Of these, the largest are the American Baptist Convention (formerly the Northern Baptist Convention); the Southern Baptist Convention; the National Baptist Convention of America (Negro); the National Baptist Convention, U.S.A., Inc. (Negro); and the Progressive National Baptist Convention (Negro). These and similar organizations of Baptists in the United States and in foreign countries are united in the Baptist World Alliance which, under normal circumstances, holds a great Congress every five years. The purpose of this assembly is fellowship, inspiration, and mutual aid.

In order that you may know something of the origin and purpose of the various Baptist organizations, let us go back in American history to the year 1638. That was a great year for our people, for in it Roger Williams founded at Providence the Rhode Island Colony. It was founded in protest against, and as a refuge from, the religious intolerance he and others had encountered in New England. It is a strange fact that the Puritans, who had come to this new world in search of religious freedom, should then deny it to all those who did not believe just as they did. Yet that is exactly what happened. In the Massachusetts Bay Colony, for instance, one had to be a member of the established church (Congregational) before he was permitted to vote as a citizen. Roger Williams believed in the principles of soul liberty and of the separation of church and state; so, when he was driven out of the Massachusetts Bay Colony and went to what is now Providence, R. I., he established there the first Baptist church in America, as well as a civil community which guaranteed religious freedom.

The Baptist movement, at first, spread slowly. When it became known that a person had become a Baptist, he was likely to suffer ridicule, persecution, fines, and imprisonment, but there were brave people who were willing to pay even that price for soul liberty. Naturally, the Baptists, who were scattered throughout the colonies, sought to keep in as close touch with one another as they could. In Philadelphia, where religious liberty had a strong foothold due to the influence of the Quakers, Baptists invited their brethren from surrounding areas to join them in fellowship meetings. After a time, these meetings were held at stated intervals, twice a year, in the spring and in the fall. Baptists met to pray together, to encourage one another, and to promote the evangelization of the unsaved. In 1707, for the first time, the Baptist churches appointed official delegates to represent them at these meetings. This association included in its membership churches from southern New England, New York, New Jersey, Pennsylvania, Delaware, Maryland, and Virginia.

About 1740 there was a quickening of religious interest in the churches of all denominations. This revival was brought about by the preaching of Jonathan Edwards and the English evangelists, John Wesley and George Whitefield, who visited the Colonies. As a result, Baptist work prospered, and many people were converted and united with the Baptist churches. Many new churches came into being and with them new associations. Among the earliest were the Charleston (S. C.)

Association, organized in 1751, and the Warren (R. I.) Association, organized in 1767. By 1800 there were forty-eight associations in America; thirty in the southern states, and eight west of the Alleghenies.

Most great movements have originated with great personalities. In 1812 Adoniram Judson and his loyal wife, Ann Hasseltine, took passage to India to become missionaries of Jesus Christ. They were the first foreign missionaries to go forth from America. In India they anticipated meeting the well-known English Baptist missionary, William Carey. The Judsons were not Baptists at the time they set sail, but on the long journey to India they studied the New Testament carefully. By the time that they had reached India, they had come to the point where they wished to become Baptists. They believed the Baptists' position to be the New Testament position; namely, that immersion was for believers only. The door in India was closed to them, so they went to Burma as a second choice; and that second choice became the greatest missionary field of the Baptists.

Luther Rice, who had gone out to India with the Judsons and who had become a Baptist, returned to America to persuade the Baptist people to support himself and the Judsons, who— now that they were no longer Congregationalists, could not expect aid from that source. He journeyed up and down the land, telling of the missionary need and of the consecrated labors of the Judsons. The Baptists responded with their gifts. Accordingly, in May, 1814, there was set up an organization known as "The General Convention of the Baptist Denomination in the United States for Foreign Missions." This was the first national Baptist organization, and it was born of a missionary impulse. The organization took place at Philadelphia; that city thereby became not only a shrine of civil liberty, but also a shrine of religious liberty. This organization later became known as the Triennial Convention, a forerunner of the American Baptist Foreign Mission Society of today. Its object has been to send the gospel into foreign lands. In pursuing this objective, it has had and is having glorious success.

In Burma, Judson and his wife labored sacrificially. After Judson had acquired some knowledge of the difficult Burmese language, he undertook the stupendous task of translating the Scriptures into the native language in order that the Burmese might read the gospel for themselves. To help him in this task, Judson had only an incomplete grammar and a brief dictionary which had been prepared by one of William Carey's sons. This work so stirred the hearts of Christian people in America that they moved to translate the Scriptures into other foreign languages that the evangelization of the world might be more readily accomplished. Other denominations felt the same need. Accordingly, in 1816, the first Bible Society in America was organized. But this interdenominational organization did not fully meet the approval of the Baptists. They felt that it did not correctly translate the many significant passages in the Bible concerning baptism. The Greek word *baptizo*, they contended, should be translated "immerse"; the other denominations would not agree to incorporate the controversial word "immerse" into translations of the Bible. So, in 1837, 390 delegates from Baptist churches in many sections of the country met in Philadelphia and organized the American and Foreign Bible Society to "pursue a faithful translation of the Scriptures."

In 1824, due to the efforts of a number of outstanding personalities—among them being Noah Davis, Samuel Cornelius, Luther Rice, and Obadiah Brown—a Baptist General Tract Society was organized in Washington, D. C. Before long, the name was changed to the American Baptist Publication Society, and the headquarters were moved from Washington to Philadelphia, where better printing facilities were available. The purpose of this new Society was stated in these words: "To promote evangelical religion by means of the Bible, the printing press, colportage, Sunday schools, and other appropriate ways." A colporter is one who distributes Bibles, religious books, and pamphlets as he travels from place to place.

Then there arose another great Baptist leader. That person was John Mason Peck, a fearless Baptist minister, who in his efforts to win men to Christ, traveled tirelessly over the country. He labored in the Middle States—then thought of as the Far West—preaching the gospel, organizing churches, and establishing schools. He and his co-worker, Jonathan Going, in 1832 organized the American Baptist Home Mission Society. Its purpose was to secure the proclamation of the gospel in the unevangelized areas of North America, to organize and sustain churches, and to establish and sustain Christian schools and colleges.

About this time slavery became the burning issue of the day. There were members of the churches who believed that it was not right for Christians to own slaves. Others tried to defend the institution of slavery from the Scriptures. Of course, the controversy boiled among the Baptists as well as among the members of other denominations. The crisis came in 1844. In the national gathering of the Baptists that year it was planned to avoid the issue as a Convention, but this decision was not observed. Instead, the Executive Board of the Convention refused to commission those for missionary work who were slaveholders. The next year the American Baptist Home Mission Society adopted a resolution that recommended a separation of the Baptist denomination into the two divisions, the North and the South. One month later, the Baptists of Virginia took the lead in organizing the Southern Baptist Convention. This rift has never been closed. The Baptists of the northern states remained in the General Convention. It then became known as the American Baptist Missionary Union, and established its headquarters in Boston.

During the course of these national developments among the Baptists, there had been organized in many states missionary agencies which today are known as state conventions. They are designed to promote missionary work in their respective areas. They help in establishing new churches and in maintaining weak ones. They assist in the work of the national convention as a whole, collect the missionary offerings of the churches, and encourage Christian education.

Then the women of the denomination determined to have a larger part in the missionary work of our fast-growing denomination. They organized the Woman's American Baptist Foreign Mission Society in 1874, and the Woman's American Baptist Home Mission Society in 1877. These Societies did not operate independently, but co-operated with the general foreign and home mission societies.

By the beginning of the new century, there was a growing feeling that a more unified form of denominational organization would be beneficial. The various national Societies in the North began to talk of uniting their efforts to raise from the churches the large sums of money called for by the expanding program of the denomination. This desire to do a greater work and at the same time to practice the utmost economy of operation brought into existence the Northern Baptist Convention. It was organized in Washington, D. C., in 1907, not to have authority over the Baptist churches, but to serve as their agent. It was composed of a majority of the Baptist churches in the North. Churches which co-operate in the work of the Convention are entitled to send delegates to the annual meetings.

The Northern Baptist Convention, at its 1950 meeting, changed its name to the American Baptist Convention. It was thought that the new name would be more in harmony with the traditions of the Baptist movement, and would bring the name of the Convention in line with the names of the various societies. All these societies have the word "American" in their names; three of them have borne the name "American" for more than a hundred years. In taking this action the Convention affirmed: "We hold the name in trust for all Christians of like faith and mind who desire to bear witness to the historic Baptist convictions in the framework of co-operative Protestantism."

The American Baptist Convention, except in cases of national emergency, meets once each year. The meetings usually are held during the latter part of May, and the place is some large, strategically located city. During the sessions, which last five or six days, the work of the many societies and the interests of American Baptists are presented, business is conducted, officers are elected, and other important matters receive attention. One of the many attractive features of a Convention is the fellowship enjoyed and the reunions that are made possible as the delegates and visitors come together from many different states. Between Convention sessions a General Council consisting of the Convention officers and thirty members elected by the Convention takes care of the business affairs of the Convention.

The officers of the Convention consist of a president, a first vice-president, a second vice-president, a general secretary, and a treasurer. The president presides at all meetings of the Convention and of the General Council, and exercises general supervision over the affairs of the Convention. In case of his absence or inability to serve, his duties are performed by the vice-president who is next in numerical order. Any member of a co-operating Baptist church may be elected as president. The president is elected by the delegates to the Convention, and serves for one year. The person holding this important office serves without salary.

The office of general secretary was created at the 1950 session of the Convention. In this office are combined, not only the duties that formerly had belonged to the corresponding secretary and the recording secretary, but duties of an administrative, representative, and correlating nature. The general secretary is nominated by the General Council and is elected by the Convention for a term of three years.

The treasurer administers the financial affairs of the Convention under the direction of the Convention or of the General Council. He receives all money belonging to the Convention, keeps an accurate record thereof, and deposits it or pays it out under the direction of the Convention or General Council. He is elected by the Convention delegates and serves for one year.

Agencies of the American Baptist Convention

One important agency of the Convention is the Division of World Mission Support. It is composed of members appointed by the various Boards and Societies of the Convention and eighteen pastors, six from each of the three Convention areas, and eighteen lay persons, six from each of the Convention areas, and representatives from various foreign-speaking Baptist Conferences.

Its work is to spread information concerning the work of the Convention and the related Boards and agencies, to encourage the churches to contribute to the budget adopted by the Convention, and to look after the proper distribution of the monies received.

A second agency is the Department of Christian Social Concern. Its membership, although smaller, is made up in somewhat the same manner as that of the Division of World Mission Support. Its purpose is to foster a better understanding of human relationships, to combat social evils, and to promote social betterment.

The American Baptist Foreign Mission Society and the Woman's American Baptist Foreign Mission Society work together to promote a program of evangelism, education, hospitalization, and social betterment in Burma, India, Assam, Bengal-Orissa, South India, Japan, Okinawa, The Philippines, Hong Kong, China, Thailand, Republic of Congo, and Europe. These are powerful agencies of your church. Through these societies you, by your missionary giving, can have part in the evangelization of the world. These organizations and their programs have been developed through years of testing and experience. In no other way could the foreign missionary enterprise be carried on so efficiently.

The American Baptist Home Mission Society has as its slogan "North America for Christ." It helps in the support of bilingual churches. It fosters work with Japanese, Chinese and Spanish Americans. It supports Negro educational centers. It operates Christian centers in many of our great cities. It promotes missions in Alaska, Hawaii, Latin America, among the American Indians and Mexicans, and in town and country areas of our nation. It assists in building new churches.

The Woman's American Baptist Home Mission Society also works along these lines. It promotes a work in Latin America and Alaska. It stresses the importance of Christian friendliness among people of other nationalities and races. Among other worth-while projects is the Baptist Missionary Training School for young women in Chicago. Through the church you are joining, you too can have a part in this great work for God.

In 1944 the Board of Education of the Northern Baptist Convention and the American Baptist Publication Society took steps to unify their work. The new agency is now called The American Baptist Board of Education and Publication. This organization aids, financially as well as in other ways, our Baptist schools and colleges. Through student pastors it gives religious help to Baptist students who are attending non-Baptist schools. It promotes, in the local church, children's work, youth work, adult work and Christian family life, missionary education, church school administration, leadership education, vacation church schools, camps and summer assemblies, university pastor and student work, Baptist schools, colleges, and theological seminaries. A great volume of Christian literature—magazines, papers, study courses, Sunday church school quarterlies, etc., are prepared and published by the American Baptist Board of Education and Publication. Many of the books bear the trade name, The Judson Press. The Board of Education and Publication promoted the purchase and development of the American Baptist Assembly at Green Lake, Wisconsin. There, workers from many states gather each summer in a series of inspiring conferences and training programs through which they learn to do better work in their home churches.

The Ministers and Missionaries Benefit Board, which is also a co-operating agency of the Convention, has provided through the gifts of interested individuals and of the churches of our denomination a retiring pension fund for ministers and missionaries when they have finished their active service. It meets the needs of those aged and worthy servants of the churches when they can no longer care for themselves.

Thus, you see, I have endeavored to give you a general picture of the workings of our denomination. Much more could be said, but these are the main features. The work of our Convention has come to its present status through a process of change which is a necessary part of progress. Organizations must change if they are to grow and meet the needs of a changing world. Numerous movements in the direction of improvement are going on constantly within the framework of our Convention. This is as it should be.

Each year delegates from your church meet with delegates from other Baptist churches near you in what is known as an association meeting. These usually last one or two days. Reports from the various churches are heard. Plans are discussed by the delegates for the betterment of the work of their churches. At the same time, the churches are given information concerning the broader work of the state convention and the national convention. Baptists have a chance to have fellowship with one another. At another time during the year, your church sends delegates to the state convention meeting which is held somewhere within the state. Here, again, the total program is considered and plans are made on a broader scale than is possible in the small, associational gatherings. Then, once a year, as explained above, your church sends delegates to the great national gathering of Baptists.

Thus you can see that when you unite with the church, you are uniting with an institution that has a world-wide program. Yet in all this world-wide work, each Baptist church retains its independence. The one obligation which rests upon it is the obligation of Christian love. No other pressure is brought to bear.

This, then, is the great work of your denomination, inspiring in its accomplishments, and divinely led of God. This, then, is your church at work. God grant that you will do your part.

QUESTIONS FOR DISCUSSION

1. To what extent is the organization of your church similar to that of the New Testament churches? If there is any variance, can it be justified?

2. What officers does a Baptist church have? What boards? What committees?

PROJECTS AND REPORTS

1. Report on the method your church uses in calling a pastor.
2. Confer with your pastor and report on his call and ordination to the Christian ministry.
3. Report on the method followed by your church in choosing its deacons.
4. Report on the method used by your church in conducting its business.
5. Make a map showing the ten foreign mission fields of the American Baptist Convention. Show the islands and Latin-American countries in which the American Baptist Home Mission Society is carrying on work.

CHAPTER VI

The Christian in Action

The Christian Life a Life of Action

The Christian life is not all action. Of course, it consists quite largely of gaining right attitudes, clear insights, and spiritual poise. These come to the one who will worship devoutly and intelligently. However, when all this has been done, there is yet more to do. Peter, James, and John, on the mountain, beheld the transfigured Christ and worshiped him; but there remained a work to be done in the valley. Of the church it is truly said, "We enter to worship and depart to serve." A newcomer had just entered the stillness of a Quaker prayer meeting. Everyone was sitting in his place quietly. Nothing was being said. Presently, the curious visitor whispered to the one seated nearest him, "When does the service begin?" "After the meeting," was the reply.

Hence, every Christian has a God-given responsibility to go into action. In the painting *Come unto Me*, Eugene Burnand, the Swiss artist, presents a stimulating challenge to young people of every age. The picture shows Jesus on one of his journeys through the countryside. He is accompanied by John; his other disciples, no doubt, are near by. Jesus has just encountered a group of young people. We are impressed at once by their eagerness to hear Jesus and by the seriousness with which they consider his words. The young man whose hand Jesus holds has made a momentous decision. He has decided to become one of the Master's disciples. He will follow the Master, whatever the cost may be. He offers himself as a learner, but he is ready also to serve the Master in any way he can. He will not hesitate or hold back when the Master says: "Go ye into all the world." At his side is a young woman. In a moment, she too will dedicate her life to the Master's service. It is in much this fashion that Jesus meets you along the road of life. He looks into your eyes, searches the depths of your soul: Will you do his bidding?

"Well," someone says, "what is there I can do?" More—much more, probably—than you think. No one really can tell how much he can do until he tries. Remember that if you ask God's help, and show your sincerity by doing your human best, God will aid you.

Responsibility to Be Informed

Now, in response to the query, "What can I do?" I should like to say, first of all, that you can be informed concerning what your church and denomination are doing, both in your community and throughout the world. We have suffered serious losses in our church and denominational life because Christians have not kept themselves informed. To be informed a member should, among other things, attend the business meetings of his church. That is where the organizational and planning work of your church is done. To be informed, one also should read the denominational periodicals, such as *The American Baptist, Baptist Leader,* and your State Convention publication. You have a responsibility, not only to be informed, but also to help in determining the policy of your church and denomination. Now that you are a member of the church, you have the same right as anyone else to speak in the business meetings and to vote on matters of church business. Who knows but what your voice and vote may mark a turning point for better things in the life of your church!

I believe that one of the most helpful things you could do would be to study and think through the total program of your church. Your fresh, new eyes, if you look carefully, may see many things that others do not see because they have been living with the situation for a long time and have come to accept it as inevitable. Every once in awhile it is well for us to rethink a church program, to ask ourselves: "Where are we going, anyway? Why are we doing this thing in this particular way? Is there a better way of doing it now?" Your thinking, speaking, and acting may help to get your church out of a rut. Is your church as effective as it ought to be in missionary work? In Christian education? In evangelism? In stewardship? Or is it just going around in circles in these matters?

Is it just going through the motions? These are questions you should ask yourself and your church. But do not be discouraged if you encounter in the church a great deal of indifference and lethargy; rather, be challenged by it.

This is the Christian in action!

Places of Service Within the Church

Now, a few words concerning some specific forms of service in which you may engage. Have you ever stopped to think how good it made you feel to be greeted by a sincerely friendly usher? It gave you a warm feeling toward the entire church. Some people think the work of the ushers is unimportant, but I believe they perform a most strategic service. They are among the first to greet the visitor and the newcomer. The way they greet a stranger may have more to do with that man finding Christ or uniting with your church than what the pastor has to say. It has been truthfully stated that a merchant will spend hundreds of dollars to create good will in the minds of the public, only to have it all lost by one rude, stupid clerk. This is just as true of a church. A church may spend hundreds of dollars and valuable time to attract people to its worship services, but one thoughtless, impolite, inconsiderate usher can render it all useless. Strangely enough, it is hard for a church to keep a corps of good, faithful ushers. You may see in ushering the possibility of an important service which you can render.

There are always bulletins and posters to be made for young people's meetings, for the pastor's sermons, for special events. Attractive, well-made posters add much to the effectiveness of your church's program. They are silent salesmen. Are you handy with a crayon, brush, pen, or typewriter? Then go into action.

How about beautifying the rooms of your church? You may not feel qualified to speak or to pray in public, but you may know how to clean, paint, or hang wall paper. Some of the rooms of the church may be in a dingy condition. Think how much it would enhance the work of your Sunday church school if the boys and girls had a clean, fresh, bright room in which to meet. Incidentally, I think the older folks would like it, too.

Because the trustees are responsible for all church property, be sure to secure their approval before you begin to carry out your plan. Only the other day I read in our state Baptist paper of certain classes which were taking the responsibility of remodeling and refurnishing their classrooms. I have known also of a skilled craftsman who, as a labor of love, fashioned for his church a pulpit and communion table of exquisite beauty. Such service is a genuine contribution to the life of your church; at the same time, it will bring blessing into your own soul.

Just as there are things you can do with your hands in a church, so there are things you can do with your voice. Music is one of the most valuable and inspiring parts of public worship. Through the harmonious ministry of music a worshiper's soul may be lifted up to God. If God has given you a talent to sing, you have a responsibility to use your voice for his honor and glory. Whatever your talent, and whether it be great or small, go into action with it for the Lord!

One of the most beautiful services a Christian can perform for his church is to call on the sick and the aged. This is a constantly recurring service, and one in which it is possible to do much good. A Sunday church school teacher arranged for her class of girls to call on an old lady who had been bedridden and neglected for many years. The teacher planned a short program of songs, Bible verses, and prayers for the bedside, and then as they left, each girl was to leave a flower. The program went through according to schedule. The girls sang their songs and quoted their Bible verses, to the accompaniment of expressions of surprise and finally of overwhelming gratitude on the face of the sufferer. When the prayers had been offered and the happy girls were leaving their flowers, her lips began to move. The teacher leaned closer. "I had almost forgotten," said the old lady, and then could not go on. "You had almost forgotten what?" prompted the teacher. "I had almost forgotten that there were beautiful girls like these. I had almost forgotten there was such a thing as music. I had almost forgotten there were flowers, and that God cared. Thank you so much for coming. Please come again soon."

"I was sick and you visited me," said Jesus. And after Jesus had said that, he explained: "As you did it to one of the least of these my brethren, you did it to me."

Go into action, Christian!

Then there is the work that can be done in connection with Home Visitation Evangelism. How did you learn of Jesus? Who talked with you about giving your life to him, becoming a Christian, and being baptized? Someone did. Suppose that person had not done so? It may be that someone is waiting for you to come and talk with him, just as someone came and talked with you. When Philip asked the Ethiopian, "Do you understand what you are reading?" he replied, "How can I, unless some one guides me?" It is still that way. A minister discovered this fact when, after preaching from the pulpit to a certain man for five years, he won him to Christ in five minutes during a heart-to-heart talk with him in his home. This is work which *you* can do. "You are my friends," said Jesus, "if you do what I command you." I have found that young people, properly trained, are able to do this kind of work as effectively as older people. Your pastor will be glad to instruct you in it. There are few things in life that render the rich returns that Home Visitation Evangelism brings. A salesman of ability, after having made several calls to win people to Christ and the church, remarked: "I have made sales amounting to thousands of dollars, but none of them gave me the thrill that I received the other night when I got my first decision for Christ through a friendly visit in the home."

The missionary work of your church affords another splendid opportunity for service. Your church is a missionary station serving at home and throughout the world. There is in your church a missionary organization or committee of some sort. This group plans and stimulates the church's missionary efforts. Remember that there are missionary opportunities in your own community, for right here in America fully half of our population is pagan! Perhaps you could help in establishing or maintaining a mission Sunday school in some needy area of your community.

During one of my pastorates, my attention was directed to an underprivileged community just outside the city limits. There was no church near. However, through the devoted efforts of a man and his wife who were members of my church, a little mission Sunday school was begun in a small, three-room house that was little more than a shack. That Sunday school grew until its attendance reached the almost unbelievable figure of seventy-five. I baptized twenty young people upon their profession of faith. Grown men and women were won to the new life in Christ. There stands in that community today an organized, thriving church, the direct result of the labors of those two people who were willing to go into action for Jesus. You might be the one to do such a thing for your church and your Savior!

A phase of the church's life that many members have not yet learned to enjoy is the raising and distributing of funds for the Lord's work. Because they do not understand that they are to be Christian stewards, or because, though they understand, they have not been faithful in their stewardship, they do not get the joy out of stewardship which they should. Quite often it is harder to find people to serve on the finance committee than on any other committee, and harder to get them to work on a financial canvass than on a religious census. But there are few places of service where a more needed work can be done. It is dedicated money which this committee handles. It is a holy trust. The finance committee should aim not only to save money wisely, but also to spend it wisely. It has the privilege of leading the church into avenues of happy and liberal giving. The pleasure one derives from participating in a financial canvass is determined largely by his own attitude of heart and mind. If his spirit is joyful and contagious, he will infect others with joy. So, Christian, go into action for the Lord's share.

In every church there is abundant opportunity to work with boys and girls, and there are few ways in which your efforts will yield greater dividends than in work with children. The Sunday church school class is the most strategic place in the church for achieving genuine, far-reaching results, if the teacher be sincere, trained, and energetic. An outstanding psychologist maintains that churches should spend less money on stained-glass windows and more on Sunday church school equipment.

A teacher with a group of children gathered about her is the perfect situation for character development, even though such a class may meet but once a week. Her desire to know and understand her pupils better will take her into their homes during the week, for one does not understand a child until one knows the home from which that child comes. The mental and emotional life of a child is like a sensitive photographic plate upon which may be printed lifelong images of good or evil. It is the duty of the church to imprint those images of good, but its program of Christian education can function successfully only when it has teachers who are willing and capable. Your church will provide training classes for you, if you are willing to avail yourself of the privilege.

Then, there are splendid opportunities to work with boys and girls not yet enrolled in the Sunday church school. The only thing that hinders a larger spread of such work is the very limited supply of people who are willing to give the time and energy necessary for its successful prosecution. A talented woman had not been a member of the church very long before she saw such a need. She proceeded, freely and voluntarily, to call in the girls in her neighborhood and to organize them into groups according to their ages. The girls responded as if by magic. Soon the influence extended into the homes and reached the fathers and mothers. Although the boys and girls would enjoy them and find them helpful, many churches do not have vacation church schools. You could help in such a school. Why not? Your pastor will open the way for you, if you are willing. Every wide-awake minister will welcome anyone who comes to him and says, "Pastor, I want to be of service somewhere. Put me to work."

Such work will bring you a blessing. In my pastor's class I had spoken of the fact that one may be drawn out of an inferiority complex by giving oneself in service for the Lord. After the dismissal, a timid lady approached me and said: "I think you must have said that just for me, because it certainly has been true in my case. I was afraid to take any responsibility in the Nursery Department when I was asked, but I decided I'd try. I want you to know it has helped me a lot. I just love to work with those little children."

Then, consider the youth groups of your church. If you are a young person, there will be a place for you in one of them.

It is essential to your success in Christian living that you associate yourself with other Christians of your own age; it is essential, because you will assimilate the ideas of the company you keep. Sometimes a young woman will bitterly exclaim, "There are no young men you can trust!" Now, she is not announcing a truth in human relations. She is merely confessing the kind of company she keeps. She needs to associate with the clean-living young people who go to church. She needs not only that association, but also the opportunities for service that an active youth fellowship affords. These are invaluable in the development of personality and in the building of Christian character.

However, I would not have you infer that I consider the interests of the young people more important than those of the adults. There are places of service for adults in the various adult organizations of your church. There are the organized adult classes of the Sunday church school, the Men's Brotherhood, and the Woman's Missionary Society. All of these provide worth-while avenues of service. Jesus comes to you and bids you today to go, work in his vineyard.

There are things you can do on your own initiative. You can show a spirit of Christian friendliness. There are many people in the world who are lonely and who need the friendship a Christian can give them. One can and should be friendly in God's house. Many people have united with a church because they found friendliness in it. J. L. Kraft, one of the country's leading merchants and a prominent and helpful Baptist layman, said to me, "Forty years ago, when the North Shore Baptist Church was just a small, struggling church, Mrs. Kraft and I united with it because it was friendly. I belonged to no church at the time, but I had professed my faith in Jesus Christ as my Savior. Mrs. Kraft was a member of another denomination. Out of courtesy to her, we visited a church of her faith first. We entered, sat down, listened, and walked out without a soul saying a word to us. One Sunday evening, when we were out walking, we chanced to pass by this Baptist church, and we heard the congregation singing. We went in. When the service was over, it seemed we could hardly get away because everyone was so friendly. We decided that that was the church we wanted to join." So do not think for a moment that you are too unimportant to be friendly. Who knows but what a spirit of friendliness on your part may be the deciding issue in someone's soul!

Places of Service Beyond Your Church

Then, outside of your church, there are many opportunities to display friendliness in ways which will bring spiritual healing. Many times Christians have won others to Christ and the church by using their friendship in the right direction. Make your friendships count for Christ. Then they will return to bless you. A young couple gave their lives to Jesus and were baptized. The very next Sunday they brought their closest friends to church with them. Before long, their friends openly professed Jesus as their Savior and Lord, were baptized, and in turn brought another couple to church with them. I do not know how long that process continued, but I do know it has great possibilities. In this way, perhaps more than in any other, the gospel of Christ is spread and men and women are won to the Kingdom. So use your friendships for Jesus.

There is another way in which you can exercise Christian friendliness outside your church. There probably are people of foreign birth living in your community who need your help. They may need assistance in learning the English language, or in adjusting themselves to our way of life. Perhaps there is a Christian Friendliness Committee in your church. Work with it, or through the Woman's Missionary Society of your church. Here is an opportunity of large dimensions. "Be ye kind one to another."

Christian, go to work!

But under no condition let your service be done in the spirit of a certain Sunday church school teacher. One of her pupils said to her playmate: "I don't believe Miss M_____ likes to teach us. I heard her tell the minister that we were her personal sacrifice to the Lord." The service must be willingly and lovingly given, if it is to be acceptable both to God and to man.

1. *Christian Living in the Home.* Here is another sphere in which the Christian must go into action. The home offers the

real testing ground. There is where we show what we really are. A little kindness goes a long way—especially at home.

The church exerts a tremendous influence for good in its own right, but it must yield place to the home as the most determinative influence in human life. From the moment a child is born it begins to assimilate the influences of the home; it is influenced by the disposition of its parents. The infant is sensitive to the way it is held, whether tenderly or roughly. A child who has known the love of a true parent will not find it difficult to understand the love of the Heavenly Father. As a general rule, if the home is Christian the child will become a Christian. But this is on the assumption that the parents' Christianity is genuine, positive, and wholesome. A child will quickly detect any hypocritical attitude on the part of his parents and will react accordingly. He will conclude that Christianity is merely a pose. The parents who discuss destructively a Sunday church school teacher, church leader, or pastor in the presence of the child may do that child irreparable harm. Above all else, the faith of the home must be sincere, intelligent, and healthy. An excessive display of religion cannot be used to cover up a moral or spiritual flaw, even if this religious show is put on unconsciously. Religion proves itself in worship and service, not argument.

A certain victim of paresis, which is a type of mental illness, believed that the Catholics and the Protestants had opposing armies and were constantly at war with each other. He believed himself to be a member of the Protestant army, and that the headquarters of the Catholic army was in a certain military camp. He had come to believe this fantasy because his mother had been a Catholic and his father had been a Protestant, and he had grown up in an atmosphere of continual bickering and quarreling over religion. He could not conceive of religion being other than conflict.

The Christian idea of the recognition of the rights of others can and should be learned in the home. Likewise, the Christian idea of the essential brotherhood of man can and should be learned in the home. And finally, one should acquire from his life in the home an unselfish conception of social service. If the religion of the home be true, with a positive system of attitudes and action instead of a negative system of prohibitions, then the child's religion will be positive, helpful, and enduring. In the home, more than anywhere else, we must examine our inner motives and see if they are truly after the mind of Christ. If not, "what do ye more than others?"

The memory of a parent's faithful prayers will remain with a child forever. Dr. E. Stanley Jones tells us that one night, through a crack in a door, he saw his mother as she engaged in prayer for him. He gazed, as it were, into her very soul. The memory and the influence of that sight never left him. Dr. George W. Truett said that he never forgot the sight of his mother praying for him and for her family in the orchard after she had finished the breakfast dishes. When she was through, she rose to her feet and came back to the house with her face shining. The sterling Christian character of the mother of John and Charles Wesley had much to do with making them the great men of God they became. The Christian home is one in which prayers are offered, whether at the beginning of the day, at mealtime, or at bedtime. The Christian home is one where there is an awareness of the presence of Christ.

Dr. G. Campbell Morgan relates that his father, when once he came to see him, walked through the house examining it carefully. "It is a beautiful home," he stated, "but there is nothing in it that would distinguish it as being a Christian home." Is there anything in your home that marks it as being a Christian home?

Christian, go into action in your home.

2. *Christian Living in the Community.* The Christian owes it to his God and to his neighbor to be watchful, articulate, and active in community welfare. He should be active in the interests of good government, concerned to promote education, vigilant concerning any encroachment upon the public welfare by evil interests.

If he is asked to serve in connection with some community project, he should count the service as a privilege, and carry out his task as a Christian citizen. If we wish our society to be Christian, we cannot afford to leave the government of civic affairs in the hands of godless men.

Let Christians come alive to the social issues and civic needs of the day. Let Christians be expendable for the kingdom of God.

Christian, go into action in your community.

3. *The Christian and His Vocation.* Furthermore, let the Christian carry his faith into his vocation, his profession, or his work. Christianity is not something that one places in a tight compartment of one's life, there to be kept segregated from everything else. It is not something that one uses only on special occasions, then puts back in the closet during the rest of the time. Christianity is to be practiced at all times; it is meant to be used in every area of life. Any other conception of the Christian life is a false one. "The kingdom of heaven," said Jesus, "is like leaven which a woman took and hid in three measures of meal, till it was all leavened." So the Christian faith must permeate the *whole* of life.

A psychiatrist, the brilliant son of a Presbyterian minister, effectively mingles the Christian principles he learned in his home with the therapy of psychiatry. A lawyer has a place for Christ in his consulting room; he respects and honors Christ's will. A doctor is an earnest Christian, and his belief in the Great Physician has enhanced his standing and ability. A merchant was very active in Sunday school work, being superintendent of one of the greatest Sunday schools of the nation. When asked how he managed to do that and take care of his business too, he replied: "My business? The Sunday school is my business!"

Many people err in omitting Christ from their vocations. Perhaps they do so because they fear that their popularity will suffer. Those who have admitted him into every area of their lives know that this is not true. A man can have but one master. If we do not have Christ in every area of our lives, we do not have him at all. Christ must have the pre-eminence. He must be Lord of all, or he is not Lord at all! "No one can serve two masters; for either he will hate the one and love the other, or he will be devoted to the one and despise the other."

So, in a real sense being a Christian is a vocation! We sometimes obscure this fact when we speak of going into full-time Christian work, the full-time work referred to being that of a minister or missionary. Actually, being a Christian can be a full-time work, even though one may be a waitress, a house-wife, a painter, or a carpenter. It is a vocation to be a Christian, a great and holy calling, just as sacred in its way as being a minister is sacred in another way. Let us look upon it as such. Let us say, "Henceforth, being a Christian will not be a part-time job in my life; it will be a full-time job. It will receive the best of me there is."

There is, however, the matter of receiving and answering a call to definite Christian work. Perhaps you are one whom God is calling to be a minister of the gospel. Perhaps God is calling you to go to the foreign field, or to direct the work of Christian education in some church. Perhaps you should be a pastor's assistant. Perhaps you should be a Christian teacher. Perhaps God is placing his hand on you for some such service in his Kingdom. If such be the case, think, pray, meditate until you know God's will and your own mind and own soul clearly.

Why should not some of our best young people give them-selves, their talents, and their minds to serve the King of kings? The churches need our best young people. Why should they not come? Why should not the need constitute, in part at least, the call? Does not God need you? Do you not have a talent you can give to God? Why should not this be the time to decide? The response should not be rashly or prematurely given, for if so, it may be regretted later. Some have thought they were called to be ministers when God intended them to be devoted and faithful deacons. What *your* calling is must be determined after careful thought and earnest prayer. In the case of any of the specific Christian callings, a young person's motives must be unselfish, for his remuneration will never be large. His aim must not be self-glory; for if it is, he will experi-ence disappointment and become a source of trouble to others who have to work with him. The attraction to the calling must not be born of a desire to be the center of interest and ad-miration, for such a desire will never be satisfied thus. Instead, he must be reasonably sure that his call is from God, and that there is something in him he can give the churches.

He must not be afraid of long, hard preparation, but rather should enter upon it with eagerness. It never has been true that the Almighty puts a premium on ignorance. Our forefathers did great things for God without formal training, but we live today in a culture in which a college education is commonplace, and in which the young minister or Christian worker must have an education the equal of, or superior to, that of the average layman, if he is to command the respect of those whom he would reach and win and hold for Christ. Christ taught his disciples before he sent them out. The young person who chooses to enter upon full-time Christian service must be willing to prepare himself to the best of his ability.

This final word: your horizon, young Christian, must be as broad as God's, as wide and as deep. The City Foursquare that John saw coming down out of heaven from God was as broad as it was high. Its latitude with men was as great as its height with God. When you enter the Christian faith, you enter a world fellowship, a fellowship that recognizes no distinctions of race, social status, or nationality. "There is neither Jew nor Greek, there is neither slave nor free, there is neither male nor female; for you are all one in Christ Jesus."

Let us so walk.

"Look forward, not backward; look upward, not downward; look outward, not inward; and lend a hand."

Christian, let us join hands with our brethren all over the world, in one mighty spiritual brotherhood. Let us throw down the barriers, that men may be free and may gather as one about the Christ.

Christian, go into action as a world citizen.

QUESTIONS FOR DISCUSSION

1. Where do you think your church needs your help? What church service are you willing to render?

2. What makes a home Christian? What in your home is Christian? How can your home be made more Christian?

3. What is your church doing to make your community Christian?

4. What were some important decisions made in the last annual business meeting of your church?

PROJECTS AND REPORTS

Let the teacher, with the help of the class, prepare an interest-finder and use it in this closing session to discover what are the possibilities of recruiting persons for Christian service.

For Further Reading

Day, LeRoy J., *Dynamic Christian Fellowship.* Valley Forge: Judson Press, 1960.

Handy, Robert T., *Members One of Another.* Valley Forge: Judson Press, 1959.

Hudson, Winthrop Still, *Baptist Concepts of the Church.* Valley Forge: Judson Press, 1959.

————, *Baptist Convictions.* Valley Forge: Judson Press, 1963.

Lumpkin, William Latane, *Baptist Confessions of Faith.* Valley Forge: Judson Press, 1959.

Maring, Norman H. and Hudson, Winthrop S., *A Baptist Manual of Polity and Practice.* Valley Forge: Judson Press, 1963.

Million, Elmer G., *You Are the Church.* Valley Forge: Judson Press, 1961.

Mullins, E. Y., *Baptist Beliefs.* Valley Forge: Judson Press, 1925.

Torbet, Robert G., *A History of the Baptists.* Valley Forge: Judson Press, 1950.

————, *The Baptist Story.* Valley Forge: Judson Press, 1957.

Vedder, Henry C., *A Short History of the Baptists.* Valley Forge: Judson Press, 1907.

Year Book of the American Baptist Convention. (Issued annually.)

0-8170-0103-4